# The Author

Fred Abrams is the co-author (with his wife Jeri) of the only book on Amazon written by an ordinary widow/widower couple on dealing with the loss of one's spouse: <u>Thanks For The Dance</u>. This book was inspired by the reaction to that book. Fred is a retired US Air Force combat experienced fighter pilot who also worked in program management and logistics during his 27 years of service. Following USAF he worked in industry in defining and maturing technology upon which business enterprises could be built - he is the named inventor on 17 patents. He then worked as a consultant and trainer in project and program management and leadership. He has also written children's books promoting the adoption of dogs from rescue shelters. He has been an active member of Rotary for over 25 years and leads his club's international projects. If you wish to communicate with Fred, his e-mail is: Fred@noxqq.com (www.noxqq.com has info on Fred's books).

Forward by Dr. Susan Hayes, Ph.D. who is gerontologist, community leader, retired healthcare executive, and writer. Her Ph.D. is in Leadership and Change and she is a long time member of Rotary with the author.

Information on Holistic Healing Applications was provided by Reiki Master/EPT Practitioner Amy Schenck. That information is near the end of Chapter 5.

Copyright 2017 Fred Abrams
(Revised 2021 in response to comments from readers)

All rights reserved. No part of this book may be used or reproduced by any means, graphic, electronic, or mechanical, including photocopying, recording, taping, or by any information storage retrieval system without the written permission of the author except in the case of brief quotations embedded in critical articles or reviews

ISBN-13: 978-0692960691
ISBN-10: 0692960694

# Introduction

The motivation to write this book grew out of the reaction to Jeri and Fred's prior book

### Thanks For The Dance:
### Transforming Grief Into Gratitude When Your Spouse Dies

which we published in 2013. That is the only book we know of on Amazon.com written by an ordinary widow/widower couple on this subject.

As we discussed the subject with others and made presentations to groups, we found a lot in interest in applying much of what we said to life in general. Following the death of a spouse, one's greatest hope is to once again find happiness in life, to be content instead of being in anguish. The earlier book refers to the journey or pathway you are on in dealing with the loss. We concluded that most people are on a similar journey in their lives and the pathway often involves reacting to the things that happen to them. The famous quotes surrounding whether the focus is on some destination or the journey itself came up multiple times and inspired the title of this book. We obviously believe there is a definable destination.

There are three levels of motivation to write this book.

1. The lowest point in my life was Nancy's death. I knew it was coming from the "3-5 years to live" diagnosis. In the aftermath I came to reflect on many things. Perhaps the deepest was that I realized that I was more alone in life than I had ever been.

As I explained in the first book, I was an only grandchild so as my grandparents and a very special aunt (childless) died I became closer to all those who knew my life story. This obviously included my mom and Nancy. It also included renewing and strengthening friendships from school. When my mom died I felt a need to make sure Nancy had seen the places important in my growing up. When Nancy died I realized that I was really alone - on the pointy end of my life's history with only my kids and friends from the past along the shaft of that spear hurtling through time. I found myself reflecting a lot on how wonderful my life had been, how blessed I had been, and how grateful I was for everything. I reflected a lot on what I had learned going through life. Gratitude for my life experiences and for the contentment I had found overwhelmed me. I tried to put a lot of that into the book to help others who found themselves where I was in hopes of helping them through that nadir. That motivation remains here.

2. After publishing <u>Thanks For The Dance</u> the feedback we got from others was amazing and made me feel I had done something that truly helped hurting people. I also became much more aware of how many people I knew didn't have the overwhelming sense of contentment that I had. I felt an almost evangelical zeal for trying to say to a broader audience all that I had said in that book plus a lot of what I felt that I hadn't put in that book. I had repeatedly shared much of this with Jeri. I wanted everyone I knew to have a chance to be as content as I had become. Jeri joked in our book about how analytical I am. It's true. I thought analytically about where my contentment came from and came up with the three-part approach in this book: relationship with God, the life you are living, and "in the moment."

I decided to break the second part into three smaller parts - retrospection, introspection and the future.

The retrospection part was particularly important since almost anyone who has lost a spouse is filled with second guessing or regrets about everything that went before. I felt it critical that anyone seeking contentment as a life destination first reflect on how they got to where they are. The introspection part also was designed to answer had the hidden question -"do you really know where you are and who you are?" I then felt that once you figure out where you are and how you got there, I should offer thoughts on how to get to where you want to be. The second half of <u>Thanks For The Dance</u> is about how you go about rebuilding your life and reinforcing the realization that the death of your spouse gives you a much blanker slate on which to write the future than you may realize. The things in that book's rebuilding discussion are the same for anyone wanting to head somewhere different. The third element, the moment, was mostly influenced by the overwhelming contentment I feel almost every day with Jeri, my rescue dogs, and the environment I now call home. I concluded that you cannot truly be content unless you can place yourself in that moment at will. I wanted desperately to share these revelations with others so they too may be as content as I am.

3. After I was well underway writing this book I came across the final element the book would accomplish. You tend to notice things that fit the pattern of what you are working on and the new questions were: "What is it that you want your kids and grandkids to know about life? What lessons that you have learned do you want to impart to them?" I found suggestions that one should write letters to them to be read after you are gone telling them what you think is most important for them to know.

So, this book has also become my message to my kids and grandkids about how they should live their lives to find contentment. A lot of this message they have already heard in pieces so it shouldn't be a revelation. The ones I love are the most important audience for what I have to say.

4. As I was writing the 2021 update, I spent a lot of time with a dear friend, Bill Yanney, a retired US Army Chaplain, who was in hospice care. He was fluent in Biblical (Kione) Greek and showed me a greater depth of understanding comes from looking at popular verses in the original Greek and the context in which their author wrote. I have added a number of Greek references to this update as a result- I hope they are as enlightening for you as they were for me.

The goal of this book is to make you stop and think about the life journey you are on and to consider that perhaps there is a destination to which your "internal Global Positioning System (GPS)" should be set.

There is another benefit from finding contentment; experts tell us that being content plays a huge part in your physical health as well as your emotional health. More and more medical research is being done and it concludes that our emotional and physical health are directly connected. Our bodies respond physically, for better or worse, to our thoughts, feelings and actions. Negativity and stress have been shown to slow down both our body's ability to heal and our immune system response causing us to get and stay sick more often and for a longer duration. Positive thoughts, emotions, and acts do just the opposite! So obviously, your body operates more effectively when you practice the forgiveness, gratitude, and loving acts suggested in this book. Love is a higher vibration than fear, anger, and other such emotions and dis-ease cannot live in a low vibration. Raising your vibration is as simple as being content and spreading the love! This aspect of giving your life's journey a new destination is addressed in Chapter 5.

I hope this offering gives you pause to consider many things.

# Forward
Susan M. Hayes, Ph.D.

If you are on a journey to enjoy life more and experience less stress and discontentment, you should enjoy reading this book. If you are anything like me, once you start reading, you won't be able to put it down. The writer has realized alignment with his God and being open to nudges to take specific paths and the benefit of positive lessons after negative experiences and values contentment and gratitude that create meaning in his own life.

My takeaway is an ability to connect the dots in my own life to enhance my happiness and re-focus on what brings me joy and bliss. My positive energy can be increased by forgiving myself for those things I couldn't get done, and forgive others for what they did or didn't do. It is amazing how dynamic the contentment level becomes when you focus on your passion.

This book is a great reminder to take the time to think about my own life's journey from time to time. To know where I am headed and most importantly to understand why it is so important to me. The author wrote this book, in part because he is compelled to tell his family why he was so passionate about specific things in his life. How bad experiences informed his level of contentment and how forgiveness helped him focus on what was most important.

In providing services in the healthcare field for many years, I have first-hand knowledge of how "what we think" affects our energy level and ultimately our health. That when we take care of ourselves and keep our stress levels under control, we can handle more complexity in our lives. When we become stressed, we react and can overreact to situations making them more difficult for everyone. There are limited resources, and we need to use them wisely.

This book reminded me to take time to reflect more often, be more grateful for my many blessings and be comfortable living in the moment. The writer asks all of us to raise our endorphin levels by laughing more, enjoying our life and being content.

# Table of Contents

# Chapter 1:

# The Destination

How many times have you heard this maxim?

## *Life is a Journey, Not a Destination*

The context is usually that we should enjoy the journey and make the most of it.

Do you believe this?

I hope so!  Life is indeed lived a moment at a time and the joy of life should be in the journey, in each moment.

If every moment of your life is focused on getting somewhere else, on achieving some goal not yet achieved, then you are, indeed, missing the joy of life.

I contend that there is, indeed, a destination for life's every moment and for life's accumulating years.

Unlike a book or story that leads you along toward some promised climax or revelation, this one gives you the answer here on page one.

### *The destination is contentment.*

There! Done!

Yes - but it's not that easy. For what is contentment?

Happy in the moment?  Yes.
Happy in retrospect? Yes.
Happy about the prospects for the future? Yes.
BUT......

To be content is not necessarily happiness or contentment.

The French phrase "Je suis content" is literally "I am content" but ask someone truly fluent in French what it means. It is more like "I have contentment." It is a full description of the achievement of contentment.


## History of the saying

Most often this saying is attributed to Ralph Waldo Emerson around 1845, but it appears it is actually a paraphrase of what he actually said, "...to find the journey's end in every step of the road..."

There have been many repetitions of this thought, mostly in the 20th century. The earliest written record of the exact saying is in 1920 in "The Christian Advocate" in an article written by theologian Lynn Hough about the teachings of Simon Peter. Similar sayings ("life is a journey, not a rest" and "life is a journey, not a home" did appear in the 1850's however). The saying does occur in the 1993 Aerosmith single "Amazing."

There is dialogue in the 2006 movie "Peaceful Warrior" that also captures the underlying thought very well "...the journey is what brings us happiness, not the destination."

One of my favorite comic strip characters growing up was Pogo. It was a strip of amazingly thought provoking philosophy. One of my favorites is:

*"Too soon we cross the finish line.*
*Too late we realize the fun was in the running."*

One of my other favorite comics was Calvin and Hobbes. There is one where Calvin says "Here I am happy and content. ...but not euphoric. So now I'm no longer content. I'm unhappy. My day is ruined. I need to stop thinking while I'm ahead." It is the danger of a book like this one - you can overanalyze something like contentment and find more reasons to be discontent. The message is both doing the things that lead to contentment and avoiding the things that impede that journey.

So, once again, the thrust of this book is that we can define a destination for our journey through life - that destination is CONTENTMENT.

Knowing early on where we are headed makes it a lot easier to plan and map the journey. Happiness in life comes from having chosen the right journey. But there is something more than just happiness. Victor Hugo, in Les Miserables, stated

*"It is not enough to be happy, one must be content."*

This is not an original thought by any means.
Alfred Nobel said it most succinctly:

*"Contentment is the only real wealth"*

The Greek philosopher Epictetus, writing around 100AD provided what we think is the best definition of wealth:

*"Wealth consists not in having great possessions,*
*but in having few wants."*

Long before Epictetus and Nobel weighed in, the Greek philosopher Socrates, circa 400BC, said:

*"He who is not contented with what he has,*
*would not be contented with what he would like to have."*

At about the same time Buddha (captured in verse 204 of the Dhammapada) said:

*"...contentment the greatest wealth..."*

And before Socrates and Buddha offered their wisdom, the Chinese philosopher Lao Tzu, writing around 550BC, offered this succinct conclusion about contentment:

*"Contentment is the greatest treasure."*

And more recently the Dalai Lama said

*"The purpose of our lives is to be happy"*

The Scottish theologian William Barclay opined that "There are two great days in a person's life - the day we are born, and the day we discover why."

So, once again, this book does not provide groundbreaking new thoughts. Its purpose is to make us reflect on wisdom long part of human civilization. The goal is to expand our understanding of what contentment means and embrace it as the destination of our lives.

Marcus Aurelius (121 -180AD) captured this same thought when he said, *"Very little is needed to make a happy life; it is all within yourself, in your way of thinking."* Our goal in this book is to stimulate reflection, expand understanding, and then change your way of thinking.

## Understanding Contentment

Consider this - Contentment is generally silent - what gets all the attention is the sound of dis-content. This biases the seeming reality since it is the discontent that gets the press and becomes the news - in individuals and in nations. The nature of reality is a deeper philosophical discussion worthy of additional study. Suffice it to say that reality is what we perceive it to be - just as putting on sunglasses changes our view of the world so the paradigms we embrace filter out inputs that don't conform to our view of reality. It is your personal set of paradigms (underlying and often unacknowledged assumptions about yourself and the world around you) that determines what makes it through to your consciousness as significant information and worthy of consideration in decision-making.

There are at least four words that seem to exist in a circular set of definitions. In my view there is a hierarchy and contentment is at the top of it. We could spend many pages going around in circles about which is imbedded in the other, but let's settle on this. Here is how I see the subtle differences in these words -

*Happiness* - generally defined as a state of well being from living a good life. Some are more specific in saying that it is a sustained state rather than jumping from one joy to the next.

*Joy* - generally defined as experiencing great pleasure or happiness. The term is used a lot by author C.S. Lewis and is the focus of a book by Desmond Tutu and the Dali Lama.

*Bliss* - a term made very popular by Joseph Campbell in the 1980's it has been variously defined as perfect happiness, great joy, or utter contentment

*Contentment* - the word that appears in most definitions is satisfaction or being satisfied. The ancient Greek terms come from the words self *(autós) and sufficiency (arkéō)*. It has been differentiated from the above words by saying that contentment is not being excitedly happy or joyful, but rather feeling a peaceful ease of mind or self-sufficiency.

Contentment is wanting or being satisfied with what you have - it is sufficient for your needs. Even if you feel that contentment is the foundation upon which happiness, joy and bliss are built, it is still a good destination for life's journey.

Look less at those who have more than you and more at those who have less. If all the wealth of the world was put in one pile and everyone had to take an equal share, chances are you would rather have what you now have. Your life is someone else's fervent dream or fairy tale life.

There is a Norwegian/Swedish word, "lagom," that captures a good approach to earthly wealth: "just the right amount." It is part of the Swedish proverb "Enough us as good as a feast." This is the opposite of "more is better." It is at the heart of the philosophy I preach - "Be satisfied with, and grateful for, all your blessings." William Blake pointed observed that "you never know what is enough, unless you know what is more than enough."

There is a 1910 book called <u>Adventures in Contentment</u>. If you can find a copy it is a great read. Some points made by the author are: Enjoy life and enjoy the enjoyment; marvel at every little thing. He relates a story of comparative happiness between a farmer and a millionaire- guess who was happier.

Achieving contentment in our life has multiple dimensions that will form the main body of this book. We contend that there are basically two things we need to focus on:

      1. Things that cause us to be content - specific places where we need to be content, to say that our life is filled with contentment.

      2. The time focus of our contentment. The past, the general present, and the "right now." Once we make it our destination we also focus on the future.

The author G.K. Chesterton said that "gratitude is happiness doubled by wonder." Gratitude is a key element of finding contentment. Being satisfied is a key first step toward being grateful. Author Sarah Ban Breathnach offered that "Gratitude bestows reverence, allowing us to encounter everyday epiphanies, those transcendent moments of awe that change forever how we experience life and the world."

Before we go into detail with our conclusions, I want to explain that this book is written by a person of faith (Christian) and hence contentment in one's relationship with God is a dimension. I would ask that non-believers NOT slam the book shut at this point or move immediately to skip past chapter two. There is an amazing amount of applicable material in the next section that applies even if the reader is an atheist. If your contentment is marred by anger, fear, anxiety, or impatience, you will find much of importance in chapter two. I have chosen to include all of these under Relationship with God because all of these, and many other feelings, are part of being content with that relationship.

The underlying motivation to write this book was to expand the audience for the thoughts in our earlier book on dealing with the loss of a spouse, Thanks For The Dance and to delve deeper into the subjects discussed there. When I was about 90% complete in writing this book, I had the opportunity to read The Book of Joy by Nobel Peace Prize winners The Dali Lama and Desmond Tutu and to spend some time in Tibet as a tourist. Both were opportunities to reflect on more diverse points of view about happiness and contentment and what I wanted to say here. I strongly recommend their book.

Why, you may ask, would a Christian author be enamored by things someone like the Dali Lama has to say or observations in Tibet. The reason is that many people reading this book and hoping to gain something from it will agree that the Dali Lama and ancient philosophers have said some wise things that are consistent with the Bible. Considering sources other than the Bible reinforces in me why I embrace it as the ultimate foundation of my life. These are universal truths that are worth considering in ones search for contentment; the Bible is the right place to look.

The dimensions of contentment I will cover in the remainder of this book are:

1. **Contentment in our relationship with God.** As a Christian I clearly think this is the most important and the Bible spends a lot of time providing guidance about how to find this contentment.

2. **Contentment in the way we have lived, are living our lives and where we are headed in life.** Here I discuss living life by satisfying our inherent preferences, doing the things that are most important to us, meeting our expectations, and defining and achieving what we consider to be success. This retrospective, introspective and forward look at our lives is consistent with the words of Socrates (circa 400BC near the end of his life):

**"The unexamined life is not worth living"**

3. **Contentment in the moment.** Here I discuss the importance of being able to find contentment even when things are going poorly or we find ourselves on a detour. One should be able to escape from temporary discontent.

# Chapter 2
# Contentment in Our Relationship with God

If you are a person of faith you know the importance of this dimension, however that importance varies widely among people. The atheist is totally content because he denies that God exists and therefore doesn't worry himself about this relationship. The believer has a much more difficult situation. I happen to be a Christian. My view of Christianity is less as a religion (man's approach to worshipping God) and more importantly a personal, scripture-driven, relationship with God - hence the title of this chapter. The word religion is rarely used in the Bible; James 1:26-27 is the strongest definition "If anyone thinks he is religious and does not bridle his tongue but deceives his heart, this person's religion is worthless. Religion that is pure and undefiled before God, the Father, is this: to visit orphans and widows in their affliction, and to keep oneself unstained from the world."

## τί ζητεῖς

This is Biblical Greek (pronounced "ti zhahtao") and are the first words recorded as spoken by Jesus in the Gospel of John. The common translation is "What Doth Thou Seek?" That is a great question for this chapter to address - one must know what one is seeking in their relationship with God to be content in its satisfaction.

## μετάνοια

This is another Biblical Greek word (pronounced "metanoia") which is used 22 times in the new testament. It has the simple meaning of changing ones mind and a deeper meaning to have the change in your heart. I hope what you read here has that deeper effect on you. (The English version is "repent.")

As a Christian I view Christianity as a belief that brings us all together, uniting us in our diversity, giving us a greater and much more significant commonality than any differences we may have. There are multiple places in the Bible where we are admonished to love one another. Again, Christianity is about uniting all of us in our love of God and our acceptance of Jesus Christ as our savior. Christianity is about community and we are told to spur one another on, to help one another deepen and live our faith. This means that we help others and also, very importantly, invite others into our lives to help us. It means we share our need for help. Stated as simply as possible, it means the relationship discussed in this chapter is not so much "me and God" but "us and God." Our shared faith brings us together as a community of believers.

Here are some things to think about as we explore this dimension and define what it is we seek to satisfy in becoming content in our relationship with God.

1. Do you believe that God guides your life? - If you truly do then there is no fear or anxiety in your life, for fear and anxiety are symptoms of not believing that God is indeed guiding your life. Most, if not all of us fall short in the "lack of anxiety" measure. It's hard to be content when you are filled with anxiety.

2. Do you believe that you have a purpose in life and do you have faith that the purpose will be reflected in the works that you will be guided to perform during your life? It is hard to be content when you aren't sure if you are seeking to follow the right path. Recall the Chapter One quote from William Barclay.

3. Do you believe that God answers your prayers for guidance and that God does indeed nudge you to move in the direction He wants you to go? Do you feel you have the ability to be aware of being nudged? It's hard to be content when you aren't sure.

4. Do you believe in the absolute sovereignty of God? Again most of us as believers will profess this, but deep down do our thoughts and actions always align with this belief? It's hard to be content when you harbor doubts.

5. Do you believe that the Bible has defined the way you should live your life and that you sin when you fail to follow that guidance? Do you recognize when you deviate from the mandated path and do you seek forgiveness? Most people think only of the "big" sins; in reality the Bible doesn't categorize sins and there are a lot of "contentment killing" behaviors that fall into this category. It's hard to be content when you feel you are sinning, and we all do, a lot!

There is an alarming trend among many believers today - it has been called "Contemporary Gnosticism" by some. It is counter to teachings of the Bible but appears to be consistent by its initial teachings. It confirms that God created all and watches over humankind, wanting them to be good to each other. It further contends that God does not need to be engaged in our daily life, but only when we call for help. It further strays in teaching that our central goal in life is to be happy and satisfied with ourselves - this is different from what I say in this book; our relationship with God is to be the foundation of our lives. God does guide our lives. Contentment in that relationship is paramount to all else.

# The Bible on Contentment

The Bible offers a lot of support for the importance of contentment.

Paul's Letter to Timothy (1 Tim 6:6-8) states:

> *"But godliness with contentment is great gain.*
> *For we brought nothing into the world,*
> *and we can take nothing out of it.*
> *But if we have food and clothing,*
> *we will be content with that."*

Paul's Letter to the Hebrews (Heb 13:5-6) states:

> **"Keep your lives free from the love of money**
> **and be content with what you have, because God has said,**
> **"Never will I leave you; never will I forsake you"**
> **So we can say with confidence,**
> **'The Lord is my helper, so I will have no fear.**
> **What can mere people do to me?' "**

If you are to be content in your relationship with God, you probably need to think a little more about the nature of that relationship. It is not something you can take for granted and be content. It is very easy to focus your contentment on your earthly existence (mortal life, a temporary body for the real you, your soul); does this really matter in the overall scheme of things? Should this book just stop with this chapter and not even talk about contentment with your earthly life?

The Bible suggests to some this is so and this can make religion "off-putting" for a lot of people. For example, further on in Paul's Letter to Timothy he seems to suggest the answer is "Yes, we should turn our focus from the material."

*"Command those who are rich in this present world*
*not to be arrogant*
*nor to put their hope in wealth,*
*which is so uncertain, but to put their hope in God,*
*who richly provides us with everything for our enjoyment.*
*Command them to do good, to be rich in good deeds,*
*and to be generous and willing to share.*
*In this way they will lay up treasure for themselves*
*as a firm foundation for the coming age,*
*so that they may take hold of the life that is truly life."*

In reality, verses like this need a closer reading in the context of other Biblical writings. What you find is that the Bible is really talking about priorities for our mortal lives and not commanding us to eschew all things material. The key is in your priorities. What are you seeking in this mortal life? Luke 12:31 hints at this, saying,

**"Seek the Kingdom of God above all else,**
**and he will give you everything you need."**

There's that word "seek." Its hard to be anxious about life if you truly believe these words of Luke. Note that it says "above all else" and not "instead of all else."

If your relationship with God is your number one priority, it is OK to climb the ladder of success in this mortal life..... so long as the ladder is leaning against the right wall.

The Bible tells us to work hard in this life and prepare, saving for the lean times. Proverbs 6:6-11 provides the following lesson familiar to most,
**"Take a lesson from the ants, you lazybones**
**...labor hard ...a little extra sleep ...**
**then poverty will pounce on you like a bandit;**
**scarcity will attack you like an armed robber."**

How can you tell you are on the right track, that your ladder to success in life is leaning against the right wall? If you follow the advice just offered, your life will be free of greed and covetousness. The Bible is pretty clear about that in several places:

> Luke 12:15 *"Beware! Guard against every kind of greed. Life is not measured by how much you own"*

> Colossians 3:5 *"... Don't be greedy, for a greedy person is an idolater, worshiping the things of this world"*

If you follow this advice, your happiness will not be driven by your circumstances. At the conclusion of Paul's letter to the Philippians, (Phil 4:10-13), he states

> *"I rejoice greatly in the Lord that at last you have renewed your concern for me. Indeed, you have been concerned, but you had no opportunity to show it. I am not saying this because I am in need, for I have learned to be <u>content whatever the circumstances</u>. I know what it is to be in need, and I know what it is to have plenty. <u>I have learned the secret of being content in any and every situation</u>, whether well fed or hungry, whether living in plenty or in want. I can do everything through him who gives me strength."*

Paul reinforces this thought in his letter to the Thessalonians, (1Thes 5:18)

> *"give thanks in all circumstances"*

The Bible (Luke 12:21) makes it clear that it is a matter of priorities and not a command to eschew earthly wealth.

> *"Yes, a person is a fool to store up earthly wealth but not have a rich relationship with God."*

What does this say? Read it again. It does not say you are a fool to store up earthly wealth! It says that doing so without the relationship with God is foolish. This is why this book says seeking contentment in your relationship with God is paramount and why it goes on in future chapters to talk about contentment in your earthly life. Surely, you can and should do both.

The writings in Hebrews 4:1-13 talk about finding the rest that God took following creation. That "rest" comes not from frenetic activity (or works) trying to please God, but rather from finding contentment in the rest that comes from placing your faith and trust in God. Entering into or experiencing that "rest" is the goal and is how one might define "contentment in your relationship with God." Those who believe and obey are able to enter what God calls "My Rest."

Jesus is quoted in Matthew 11:28-30

> *"come to me and I will give you rest*
> *and you will find rest for your souls."*

While it would be fitting to say that this refers to a life beyond, it is equally valid to say that an earthly sense of security and peace is what it means and feels like to be content in your relationship with God.

## Dis-Content and Its Relationship to Sin

What keeps you from being content?
Easy Answer- discontent.

But discontent with what? Your circumstances? Your spiritual growth? With Injustices you see or experience? With evil in the world or around you?

Discontent is not an end in itself. It is the entry and ending point for a number of things more recognizable as sins such as resentment and bitterness.

Since this chapter is on your relationship with God, you need to ask yourself why you are not fully content with that relationship (if indeed you are not fully content).

We talked earlier about fear and anxiety. Do you fear that you have not/are not leading the Christian life you should? Do you think you sin? Is there a relationship between your anxiety and your sins? Are you truly part of a community of believers all dedicated to helping one another in our faith?

One of the things that is a real turnoff to people newly coming to a life of faith is the constant harping by religion on sin. It is a fact that trying to avoid sin and asking forgiveness for it is fundamental to Christianity. A lot of folks think about the "big sins" and stop there. What are those big sins? The "Thou Shalt Nots..." and the things that will bring us into scandal and shame. Most people don't think a lot about the "little sins" - those things that lead to discomfort. They think even less about the things we do every day that are counter to the Bible's teachings.

So, is there really a hierarchy of sins?
What does the Bible say about categorizing sins? James 2:10 provides the answer:

*"For whoever keeps the whole law
and yet stumbles at just one point
is guilty of breaking all of it."*

That's a pretty tough standard!! Note that it says law and not laws! That would say that there is no hierarchy of sins. So sinning is sinning and we are expected to recognize all the sins and ask forgiveness in all instances.

We don't need to recount all the "Thou Shalt Not" sins, but it is worthwhile talking a little about the other things the Bible considers sinning. What is most significant about discussing these things is how they tie into our being discontented. The Bible is pretty clear about the importance of being grateful in all circumstances; not just 1Thes 5:18 mentioned earlier, but also Ephesians 5:19-20.

> *"Sing and make music from your heart to the Lord,*
> *always giving thanks to God the Father for everything..."*

So it certainly appears that not being always grateful and giving thanks violates Biblical guidance. It could be considered sinful to not be grateful enough. Luke 17:11-19 provides a story worth thinking about. In the story, Jesus heals ten lepers and only one thanks Jesus for the healing. Jesus says to the one (who is a Samaritan, a foreigner in the land),

> *"Were not all ten cleansed? Where are the other nine?*
> *Has no one returned to give praise to God except this*
> *foreigner?"*

Surely the blessings we receive from God are not as great as received by these lepers. Jesus is surprised that only one has given thanks. Praise to God is expected. It would certainly appear that not being thankful is a sin.

How many of the following have been part of your life: Pride, Selfishness, Lack of Self-Control, Impatience, Being judgmental, Being Envious or Jealous, or Speaking wrongly? Most would plead guilty to at least one.

How about pride?

You are prideful when you feel superior to others (moral self-righteousness over those who commit scandalous sins). The parable of the Pharisee in Luke 18:9-14 is a good example. Luke specifically states that Jesus told this to those who were confident of their own righteousness and looked down on everyone else. The Pharisee thanks God that he is not like all the others - who he categorizes as evildoers. Among those he calls out is the tax collector, but the tax collector asks forgiveness from God for his sins while the Pharisee is denying he sins. Jesus says:

> *"For all those who exalt themselves will be humbled,*
> *and those who humble themselves will be exalted."*

You are prideful when you believe your religious doctrine is superior to that of others - I know the "right" way.

1Corinthians 8:1 addresses holding your convictions with humility:

> *"We know that we all possess knowledge.*
> *But knowledge puffs up while love builds up"*

You have pride of achievement (your own or that of your children). Remember Proverbs 13:4 which says the lazy want much and get little, but that prospering and achieving through diligence and hard work is good. How can this kind of pride be sinful? The answer is Deuteronomy 8:17-18.

*"You may say to yourself,*
*"My power and the strength of my hands have*
*produced this wealth for me."*
*But remember the LORD your God,*
*for it is he who gives you the ability to produce wealth..."*

So it is not wrong to be proud of what you have achieved so long as you acknowledge the source of your abilities. Wanting others to recognize you for what you've achieved is also being prideful. It is not wrong to want to be recognized or appreciated (remember Jesus and the ten lepers earlier -"Were not ten cleansed?") Not giving credit/praise to God is sinful.

How about Selfishness?

The Bible is pretty specific about not being selfish.
**Philippians 2:4** probably says it best:
*"Let each of you look not only to his own interests,*
*but also to the interests of others."*

Note that this does not say to disregard your own interests but implies that we should be concerned with our own welfare **and** the welfare of others.

There are many ways that people display their selfishness.

We most immediately think of money and not using some of what you have to help others who truly need the help. There are other more subtle forms of selfishness. How about guarding your own time as valuable while imposing our demands on the time of others? You are being selfish when you are inconsiderate of others - not really thinking through the impact of your actions on others. You are also selfish when you are indifferent to the feelings of others.

Are you being selfish when you always want to be on top and to win, especially at someone else's expense? Is being competitive also being selfish?

1Corinthians 9:24-25 gives us the answer.

> *"Do you not know that in a race all the runners run,*
> *but only one receives the prize?*
> *So run that you may obtain it.*
> *Every athlete exercises self-control in all things.*
> *They do it to receive a perishable wreath, but we an*
> *imperishable."*

Think about this! We run the races in this human life to win things or prizes that are perishable and that is fine. So competition is fine. The end of the verse, somewhat subtly, sends the real message that this life is not a race where there is only one prize - all of the prizes of this mortal life pale in comparison to the prize we win by living a God-centered life. And, everyone can win that prize. But the question that opens this paragraph asks more than just prevailing over someone else when it mentions "someone else's expense." The answer is not a clear "OK to compete and win," but rather a "win the race while not unjustly hurting the welfare of others." Not everyone is going to win the perishable prizes of this life, some will win those prizes and some will not. And, in the end, it matters little who won or didn't win them.

What about Lack of Self-Control?

The Bible is filled with admonitions to exercise self-control.
> **Proverbs 25:28** says, *"A man without self-control is like a city broken into and left without walls."*

The preceding section reminds us that the athlete (competitor) exercises self control. There are multiple admonitions to control one's desires, cravings and emotions.

**Titus 2:11-12** tells us, *"For the grace of God has appeared that offers salvation to all people. It teaches us to say "No" to ungodliness and worldly passions, and to live self-controlled, upright and godly lives in this present age."*

But also, controlling your temper - getting angry.

**Proverbs 14:17** advises self control in getting angry - *"A quick-tempered person does foolish things, and the one who devises evil schemes is hated."*

**Ecclesiastes 2:10-11, written by Solomon, generally considered one of the wisest of all men,** relates the folly in indulging oneself:

> **"I denied myself nothing my eyes desired;**
> **I refused my heart no pleasure.**
> **My heart took delight in all my labor**
> **and this was the reward for all my toil.**
> **Yet when I surveyed all that my hands had done**
> **and what I had toiled to achieve,**
> **everything was meaningless, a chasing after**
> **the wind;**
> **nothing was gained under the sun."**

What about Impatience?

Impatience usually means that we are annoyed at the faults and failures of others, even when unintentional. If God is perfect Love then 1 Corinthians: 13 tells us "Love is Patient."

But more generally see Ephesians 4:2 -
> *"Always be humble and gentle.*
> *Be patient with each other,*
> *making allowance for each other's faults*
> *because of your love."*

See also Colossians 3:12.

*"Therefore, as God's chosen people, holy and dearly loved,*
*clothe yourselves with compassion, kindness,*
*humility, gentleness and patience.*
*Bear with each other and forgive one another*
*if any of you has a grievance against someone.*
*Forgive as the Lord forgave you."*

So, are you impatient? How often? Sometimes? A Lot?

What makes YOU impatient?
> A circumstance?
> A person's failings or shortcomings?

## What about Being Judgmental?

Why are we judgmental?
> - Perhaps we equate our opinions with TRUTH.
> - Perhaps we see ourselves occupying the moral high ground or feel we have superior knowledge.

Take a look at Romans 14:4. When we judge we are taking the natural role of God.
> - But what about Moral Depravity (Romans 1:24-32, 2Tim 3:1-5) - we are commanded to avoid such people. God and the Bible is judging - we are just agreeing; BUT in agreeing we must acknowledge we too are sinners.

## What about being Envious or Jealous?

Exhibiting Envy and Jealousy can extend all the way to resentment and covetousness.
What do we envy?
> - Generally, those with whom we most closely identify and the areas that we value most.

Jealousy leads to Rivalry (our fear that our rival will become equal to, or superior to us).
- Recall the Jews of Antioch toward Paul (Acts 12:44-45)
- Recall the feelings of Saul toward David (1 Sam 18:7)

<u>What about speaking wrongly?</u>

The Bible refers to this as Committing Sins of the Tongue

Matthew 12:36 tells us
> *"I tell you, on the day of judgment*
> *people will give account*
> *for every careless word they speak"*

James 3 tells us:
> *"But a tiny spark can set a great forest on fire.*
> *And among all the parts of the body,*
> *the tongue is a flame of fire.*
> *It is a whole world of wickedness,*
> *corrupting your entire body.*
> *It can set your whole life on fire,*
> *for it is set on fire by hell itself.*
> *People can tame*
> *all kinds of animals, birds, reptiles, and fish,*
> *but no one can tame the tongue.*
> *It is restless and evil, full of deadly poison."*

<u>Some summary thoughts on sin.</u>

This section has served a dual purpose talking about things the Bible cites as sinful while showing that those same things plant the seeds of discontent in our lives. If the destination of our life's journey is to be contentment - it looks like avoiding those things the Bible says are sins helps us reach that destination even if we don't view them as sins. If one is <u>seeking</u>, as this chapter suggests, contentment in one's relationship with God, then avoiding these sins serves double duty.

## Discontent and its relationship to Anger.

Clearly being angry is incompatible with being content. You might wonder why this discussion is here, rather than under the prior section on sins. We'll explain that shortly.

First, with respect to anger, there is a body of thought that considers anger as always being a secondary emotion. This means you chose to be angry because of some other emotion that is experienced first. For example, you may be disappointed at someone - then become angry with them or embarrassed by someone - then become angry with them. Anger can also be considered the "fight" (as opposed to "flight") response to fear. It is also common during grief - you can be upset that you experienced this loss and then try to affix blame, even on God. It is not unusual for someone who has lost a loved one to be angry at God because their prayers for intercession were not answered.

Think about it. Can you remember a situation where you have gone immediately to anger? There is almost always some underlying or trigger emotion. It is not unusual to be angry with your kids over something; say they come home much later than agreed. The primary emotion is worry that something has happened to them or disappointment that they failed to live up to an agreement. Is it possible that your anger can result from something the Bible considers a sin? Sure - think about impatience discussed above.

Is anger a sin? Lets see what the Bible has to say.

The Bible recognizes that WE WILL feel anger.

> **Proverbs 16:32** says - *"Whoever is slow to anger is better than the mighty..."*

**Proverbs 29:11** says -"*A fool gives full vent to his anger, but a wise man keeps himself under control.*"

Read those quotes again.

They don't say the wise man will not be angry; they say he is slow to anger and that he keeps his anger under control.

This same thought is reinforced in

Ephesians 4:26 which says *"In your anger do not sin - Do not let the sun go down while you are still angry."*

The command is not to "avoid anger" (or suppress it or ignore it) but to deal with it properly, in a timely manner. There is no question that the Bible expects us to be angry.

Remember the story of Jesus at the temple when he cleared it of the moneychangers and animal-sellers? What emotion was he showing as he overturned tables? Right... anger.

The story is so significant that it is told in three of the gospels - **Matthew 21:12-13; Mark 11:15-18;** and **John 2:13-22**. John describes Jesus' emotion as "zeal" for God's house (**John 2:17**).

Hence his anger was a secondary emotion and it was justified. That is not the only example of Jesus being angry. Recall the story of Jesus at the synagogue of Capernaum when the Pharisees refused to answer his questions,

**Mark 3:5** says *"He looked around at them in anger, deeply distressed at their stubborn hearts."*

Distress at their lack of understanding led to anger.

Many times, we think of anger as a selfish, destructive emotion that we should eradicate from our lives altogether. However, the fact that Jesus did sometimes become angry indicates that anger itself, as an emotion, is amoral. This is borne out elsewhere in the New Testament. We need to focus on why Jesus was angry. Was there anything selfish or personal in his anger? No, not really. What was the focus of the anger? It was on sinful behavior.

When we get angry, too often we have improper control or an improper focus. We fail in one or more of the above points. This is the wrath of man, of which we are told in

> James 1:19-20 - *"Everyone should be quick to listen, slow to speak and slow to become angry, for man's anger does not bring about the righteous life that God desires."*

Jesus did not exhibit man's anger, but the righteous indignation of God.

So lets consider both sides of anger - what causes you to be angry and where does your anger take you. Think for a moment before continuing - What makes you angry?

Do you become angry when you are delayed?

Impatience is one of the most common causes of anger. Think back to the previous section in this chapter. Both Ephesians 4:2 and Colossians 3:12 tell us to be patient with others. You will encounter people who seem to move much more slowly than you'd like. Does your impatience with them cause you to feel angry? This is pretty common - if you have seen the movie "Zootopia" the feeling is captured in the scene at the Department of Motor Vehicles (DMV) where all the workers are sloths. If you haven't, you probably still get the picture.

Maybe you get angry in situations where you can't really direct your feelings at a person. Stop for a moment and take a look at the cover of this book. Imagine yourself driving along a narrow winding road, say in the English countryside, and you encounter this. Will you be impatient at being delayed? Will your impatience turn to anger? Fight off the feelings of impatience - just relax in the moment. Don't let impatience lead to anger - recognize where you are and prevent the transition into anger. (I lived in the English countryside for over four years and have encountered this multiple times. At first I was impatient, but I learned to "chill and go with the flow." It made me much more content - which is why this cover was chosen for the book.)

Do you get angry when you find someone has lied to you or broken a promise? The underlying emotion is likely disappointment, either in them for their action or in yourself for having trusted them. Anytime someone betrays trust we feel upset. If you allow this to progress to anger, what form does it take? How can you keep this situation from not triggering anger?

Do you get angry when you feel you have been treated unfairly - either by a person or by "the system." How about when bad things have happened in your life and you think "how could life be so unfair to me?" Do you get angry when you see your fundamental values violated? Think back to earlier in this chapter when we talked about being judgemental. Are the values being violated those that spring from your trust in the word of God.

What we found there is that the Bible allows for agreeing with God that his word is being violated. I must share a personal story here because I find myself trying hard to explain or rationalize the only time in my life I felt absolute raging anger.

During the time I was flying combat as a fighter pilot in VietNam, I was also the squadron Civic Action Officer - responsible for organizing efforts in support of an orphanage, a school and a leper colony. One morning we were informed that the VietCong had roughed up the nuns and kids at the orphanage the night before and told them there would be more of the same if they continued to accept help from the Americans. I have never been so angry in my life, before or since. On the combat mission I flew that morning I had confirmed kills of enemy soldiers. I was jubilant! Were these the same people who had roughed up the kids - not likely, but they represented them in my mind. The superb book The Code of The Warrior points out the sobering opinion of most that the warrior is not someone who enjoys killing. It has been over 50 years since that day and the memory is still vivid of what it feels like to have enjoyed killing.

Can you say you have ever been that angry? I still grapple with the feeling at having some of my most fundamental values violated. I want to believe that God was just as angry with those evil people who hurt the kids as I was! St. Thomas Aquinas opines that "Vengeance is... virtuous to the extent that its purpose is to check evil." That helps a little.

Try to minimize our anger and all the things it lead to.

How?

    1. Try to practice true forgiveness of others
    2. Don't let anger control you
    3. Don't do things when angry that you will later regret.

And don't forget where anger leads. To resentment? To Bitterness? To Anger based behavior (either polite or hostile)? To holding Grudges? To getting revenge? None of these are compatible with a content life.

## Can We Truly Live a Life of Contentment?

### Oh Oh ! We all sin!

So how can you be content in your relationship with God?

> 1. Recognize that you sin. Christianity is founded on repentance.
>
> 2. Offer prayers of thanksgiving to a gracious God that forgives your sins
>
> 3. Pray for guidance/wisdom to make wise, non-sinful decisions.
> 4. Be part of a community of believers all of whom are dedicated to helping each other mature in their faith. (Remember, this is about "us and God"). Help others and allow others into your life to help you.

If you are a Christian you know the answer. Seek forgiveness for your sins recognizing that forgiveness comes from accepting Jesus as your Lord and Savior. You enter into a personal relationship with God. As in any relationship each party brings something - here you bring sin and foolishness while Jesus brings forgiveness and wisdom. If you are not a Christian, think about how you become content in your relationship with God given that you do things you know you shouldn't. If you are a non-believer, ask yourself if you can truly be content knowing that you are doing such things.

## So... How About Anger

Note, again that the Bible recognizes that WE WILL feel anger.

**Proverbs 29:11** was quoted above and bears repeating here:
> *"A fool gives full vent to his anger, but a wise man keeps himself under control."*

We should try to minimize our anger and all the things it leads to.

So how does one do this?

> 1. Try to practice true forgiveness of others (forgive and forget, or is it really " but don't **you** forget that **I** forgave and forgot!") Refer to the following:

> > **Colossians 3:13** - *"Bear with each other and forgive one another if any of you has a grievance against someone. Forgive as the Lord forgave you."*

> > **Ephesians 4:32** - *"Be kind and compassionate to one another, forgiving each other, just as in Christ God forgave you."*

> > **1Corinthians 13:5** [love] *"keeps no record of wrongs."*

> 2. Live by **Ephesians 4:26** - And "don't sin by letting anger control you." "Don't let the sun go down while you are still angry, for anger gives a foothold to the devil. "

> 3. Don't commit sins of the tongue, which is easy when impatience makes you angry.

## How about Fear and Anxiety?

Do you really believe that God is guiding your life?

If so, what do you fear and what are you anxious about?

> Romans 8:31 *"What, then, shall we say in response to these things? If God is for us, who can be against us?"*

Do you believe, as I do, that I am being guided to make responsible decisions (I pray often for guidance and wisdom) and need have no fear of or anxiety about the future.)

The word fear is used frequently in the Bible. In all but one case the original Greek word is φόβος (pronounced phobos) and carries the meanings one would expect: panic, alarm, dread or desire to withdraw or flee. (Clearly it also carries the connotation respect for something/someone very powerful). The single use in the Bible of the Greek word δειλία (pronounced delia) in 2 Timothy 1:7 and is a very different word with a much richer and complex meaning. It is reticence or timidity when facing a struggle where one has a duty to act and be a part of a struggle. In combat this type of fear would be called cowardice. Ponder the next time you feel fear if you should actually be engaging and assure you are not one of the timid. It all comes down to your values and what you "should" do discussed elsewhere.

Think about the long ago nadirs (low points) in your life.
> What can you say about them now?
> Were you fearful?
> More about this in just a minute.

## How about Impatience?

1. Do you find that being impatient makes things better? Or does it lead to stress, frustration, and perhaps anger?

Does impatience cause you to commit sins of the tongue? Do you belittle people when you are impatient with them? Follow the advice of Ephesians 4:29 -

> *"Do not let any unwholesome talk come out of your mouths, but only what is helpful for building others up according to their needs, that it may benefit those who listen."*

2. Think of an experience where you were impatient and were able to realize that there was nothing you could do to change the circumstance. Think about my encounter with sheep in the road mentioned earlier.

## Is God Guiding Your Life?

Do you really believe this to be so?

Most Christians would instinctively answer yes and profess the sovereignty of God. (Proverbs 16:9 tells us that we make our plans while God guides our steps) Deep down inside, do you behave and react to life's events as though this is true? If you truly believe this, then why worry about things that go wrong?

This type of discussion makes most people uncomfortable in that they know what they should profess, but they need to live life as it comes at them with its ups and down, its disappointments, its setbacks to what we had hoped and planned for, and its catastrophes. In reality, as human beings, it is virtually impossible to face every obstacle and say, in real time, that it must be God's will.

I want to propose an exercise at this point to help you grapple with this point. Think of some of the absolutely low points in your life (what we mathematicians would call nadirs - the lowest point or points. In life it refers to the lowest point in one's spirits or fortunes).

Assuming you are old enough, pick out your life's nadirs that are at least 25 years in the past - pick out two to four of them.

> Think about those times when pain and
> suffering were so intense that it made the rest of
> life seem positively joy filled.
>
> Think about how you felt during each of them -
> put good descriptive words around them,
> devastated, hopeless, or other words of your
> choosing.

Once you have thoroughly relived each of them in your mind, think about how your life today, who you are today, is different as a result of the event. I think you will be surprised to discover that, with a quarter century retrospective, there was a positive impact on your life. While this may not convince you totally of God's sovereignty in guiding your life, I am certain that it will give you a new perspective on your life's nadirs and change how you feel when facing low points in the future. Recall the Biblical story (Genesis 50:20) of Joseph - his conclusion was that **"God meant it for good."**

Let me illustrate this exercise with my own experience. In my own life I have had four clear nadirs. Three of them happened more than 25 years ago and I have a clear understanding of how they changed my life and defined who I am. The fourth was less than 25 years ago (2004) and I find myself conjecturing on how it will turn out just like the other three.

<u>Nadir #1: The Event:</u> I was 10 years old when my dad abandoned our family. My parents, married in their early twenties, had been married for 20 years. At the time I knew he was often displeased with my mom and had been cheating on her. I would understand later in life that his displeasure was his sex life - not enough and not exciting enough. I also overheard arguments between my mom and dad concerning his displeasure and disappointment in his only kid - me. That came from his desire for a son interested in sports and anxious to do athletic things weighed against his statement to my mom, "all the damn kid wants to do is read books." I would understand later that he left my mom and married a nymphomaniac (who he couldn't keep satisfied and who started cheating on him) who he later divorced. My mom and I struggled financially below the poverty level for an extended period.

    <u>The Results:</u>

        • I promised myself in my teens that I would not get married until I was 30  so that I would never wonder what I had missed and that I would never allow sex to be so important that I would upend my life over it.

        • I also promised myself that I would encourage my own kids in the things they loved and the talents they had. In retrospect, I believe this made me a better husband and father.

        • Later in life I forgave my father for what he had done. It was one of the most freeing experiences I have had. No longer did I harbor disappointment, resentment or anger over what he had done. No longer was I, myself, a prisoner of those feelings. The teachings of the Bible on forgiveness came alive for me.

• The experience also molded my attitudes about being frugal and saving. I saved and invested some amount every single month of my working life (starting at age 14). I endeavored to impart this attitude to my own children and other young people I encountered.

Maybe I would be the same person had my dad not left us, but I know that his actions assured I would be who I am.

Growing up in a single parent home with divorced parents gives me a score of "1" on the Adverse Childhood Experiences (ACE) exam. This evaluation looks at the lifelong impacts of ten traumatic stressors. It is worth your time to search for more information on this study - it is eye-opening information about events that influence our health and resilience for the rest of our lives. It is estimated that 12% of people have a score of 4 or higher and deal with it forever.

Nadir #2: The Event: When I was a fighter pilot in VietNam I injured my back and underwent unsuccessful surgery in VietNam (post-op spinal infection dissolving my spine) ending up being airlifted to Japan and then back to the USA in a body cast. Flying fighter aircraft was the great passion of my life, and I couldn't believe they actually paid me to do it, so being out of the cockpit was a real low point. This was compounded as the recovery progressed with the expectation that not only would I never return to a fighter cockpit, but that I might be discharged from the Air Force and might never walk without pain again. I was truly laid low by this and prayed. The back healed and walking was pain free - I was grateful!
Over a period of several months the USAF decided that I could stay on active duty and that I would be sent to my fighter squadron base of choice in England, although not to fly.

When I got there, they decided to process a medical waiver to get me back in the cockpit. In short order I was back in a single-seat fighter doing all the things I loved. I met the woman who would become my wife and moved into a centuries old cottage in the English countryside. Yes - there was a lot be grateful for!

The Result: What happened here was one of the most transformative events of my attitude toward life and its events! Gratitude became the focus of my like. Every day, sometimes multiple times a day, I reflect on how grateful I was for the way things turned out. I daily offer prayers of thanksgiving for my life and every single thing that has happened. My life became one of living the Biblical admonition mentioned earlier to be thankful *in all circumstances*. Today I still make gratitude and thankfulness the foundation of my life. I seek reasons to be grateful in challenging times. I believe I have been transformed into a very different person that I would have otherwise been. God certainly meant all this for good.

Nadir #3: The Event: While flying fighters in England, as I mentioned, I met and fell in love with a USAF nurse named Nancy. We had both decided early on in our lives that we would wait until about age 30 to get married and then to devote our lives to raising a family. We married when I was 29 and we set about to start a family. Nancy was pregnant within six months, but miscarried at about 12 weeks. Six months later she was pregnant again and miscarried again at 12 weeks. We prayed for the result we wanted; our prayers were not answered. This happened twice more and the experts told us that four miscarriages in a row gave us a near zero chance of ever having children. In our thirties we were desperate to start our family and found that the timeframe for action on our adoption applications was 2-3 years.

We were devastated! A relative reminded us that, while we were stationed (military) in Ohio, we were legal residents of Illinois. As a result we put in an application in a small Illinois county and were surprised when a couple of weeks later they asked to do the home study driving from Illinois to Ohio. At the end of the visit on a Wednesday they said they thought we'd make good adoptive parents and would we be interested in a six month old boy we could pick up on Friday. Picking up our son Geoff was, for both of us, the happiest day of our lives and we headed to our parents' home so everyone could meet him. Nancy got pregnant a fifth time that weekend and nine months later our daughter Amy was born. Right now you are thinking - yeah I've heard of that happening before, but there are some other twists to the story. Why did the adoption happen so fast? The county had to do an out of state adoption due to the abused child being taken by the court from the single teenage mother and they were pondering how to go about this as we walked into their office and said "hi, we're from out of state and want to apply to adopt." But there is more. The life our son would have likely lived would likely have been one of welfare or manual work. It turned out he has an IQ above 150 and we were able to encourage him to make the most of it.

    <u>The Result:</u> Besides the obvious things in this story like gratitude for our two children and the opportunity we could offer Geoff, the mathematician in me says the chances are essentially zero that we would show up just when the agency needed an out of state adoption; that the child needed a home that valued intelligence, education and work; and that with the miscarriage history, we would immediately have our own child. Reflecting on all this has convinced me that my life     is being guided and that God is sovereign. Coupled with the overwhelming sense of gratitude I feel, I also know that good will come out of any other nadirs in my life.

<u>Nadir #4: The Event:</u> This happened about 17 years ago, so the full 25 year retrospective isn't available. After 30 years of marriage to Nancy with both our children off on their own, she was diagnosed with a rare autoimmune disease that impacted her lungs. She was given 3-5 years to live. After doing everything possible, including things that resulted in horrible side effects, she died three years later. Losing your spouse is one of the worst imaginable things that can happen to you (I think losing a child would be the only thing worse). The emotions that flood your existence are debilitating - doubt about what you should have done differently, anger at doctors who misdiagnosed the symptoms for 4 years, loneliness, and attempts to hide all those with frenetic activity. I felt the need to get into a grief support class and was told that it was too soon after her death for it to really help - I should meet with a counselor and sign up for the class starting six months later. I don't often feel compulsions, but I knew I had to be in the next class against their advice. They acquiesced.

<u>The Results (so far):</u> Clearly I don't know for sure the long view on nadir #4, but I conjecture a lot because I know that God is guiding my life.

What I did know was that the answer to dealing with this loss was to try to transform my grief into gratitude for what I had and what I was left with. I focused my total being on being grateful "in this circumstance" and on getting as much benefit as possible from the grief class of seven people I had forced myself into. In the class was a widow, Jeri, with two young adult boys; they were more lost than I was. We dated, fell in love and got married a year after we met. We both felt an almost evangelical zeal to help others who had lost a spouse.

This led us to write the only book on Amazon.com written by an ordinary widow/widower couple on dealing with the loss of a spouse. The title <u>Thanks For The Dance: Transforming Grief into Gratitude when your spouse dies</u> was inspired by a song, The Dance, that explains how one could have avoided the pain, but would have missed the dance. So again, I don't know what God's plan was in taking Nancy from me, but I conjecture that it has something to do with helping others via our book and helping guide two young men to successful careers (now an emergency medicine MD and an engineer). I believe it may be to use the pain and suffering I endured to somehow lessen the pain and suffering of others who now find themselves where I was. I think the motivation to write this book is in there somewhere as well.

I hope that by sharing some of my own life experiences you have stopped to think about your own. Hopefully you have gone back to reflect some more on your own life's nadirs and are seeking a better understanding of how they changed your life. I am thoroughly content in my relationship with God and convinced of His sovereignty. I am overwhelmed daily with feelings of gratitude for all the blessings that God has given me. I am confident and un-worried about what comes next in my life.

If you do believe that your life if being guided positively, then you likely also believe that there are things that confirm this to you. I would suggest that you accept that you will feel nudges to do something - you need to listen to these more and more and where feasible, follow them. I am convinced they are real.
It is also important to look at events that are unlikely and reconsider whether they are coincidence or chance. Some may call these "nudges" by the term intuition.

We will talk about the nature of intuition later in this book, but for me these nudges are the still, small voice we are listening for answering my prayers asking for guidance. God's Will takes has two dimensions (proscriptions- don't do this / prescriptions - do this) in guiding our lives.

Let me offer a few thoughts on nudges:
  You can categorize nudges
    • Consistent with my deeply held values (e.g. God's will) - Do It.
    • Not consistent - Don't Do It
    • Unknown - will only know in retrospect

  (If your values are aligned with God's will for us: this means that you worship Him, love him, praise him, give him thanks for his gifts; you love your neighbors, help the poor, are faithful to our spouses; you gather with other believers.)

  If unsure - wait and assess the nudge. In making a decision to follow the nudge a little lesson in Jungian Psychology may be useful- we make decisions using two different methods (reflected in Myers Briggs types)

    1) We apply Logical Analysis.
        Pro=consistent with God's will.
        Con= not
    2) We use gut feel about the action.
        Pro= it is consistent with the values and beliefs we hold dear, those which define your humanity and love of God.
        Con= it is not consistent

The key is to listen for the answers. My stories above describe several situations - Nancy and I felt compelled to seek out an out of the way adoption agency that just happened to be in need of someone from out of state; the son we adopted needed us as much as we needed him - were we guided to that time and place? Was the grief of four miscarriages and near zero likelihood of a successful pregnancy part of God's plan for us and our son? Was my compulsion to be in the next available grief class just a whim or was I being nudged?

If you are still doubting the incidence of improbable stuff in my life let me offer a couple of more:

1. Adopted son Geoff, after he got married, carefully planned when they would have their first child. Eight years later there was still no pregnancy. Geoff and I were on a flight out of Moscow that lost pressurization and had to return to the airport. Sitting in the departure area with other passengers he noted a number with young Russian children and struck up conversations. He and his wife subsequently made the decision to adopt from Russia and 18 months later went to pick up their daughter from the orphanage. His wife got pregnant while on that trip and nine months later had their son. How likely that he would have the exact same experience that Nancy and I had?

2. When Nancy was close to death, the last thing she heard was Geoff saying that his wife had just called to report she was pregnant, letting Nancy know they were about to repeat our experience. As she died shortly thereafter, my daughter's 14 month old daughter looked up and said "mammaw. No, back, back. No. K. bye-bye mam-maw." What did she experience? Clearly she had no understanding of what was happening.

3. After Jeri's two sons were out on their own, we decided to downsize and started looking in a county area not far from us. Driving past a for-sale sign along a road we'd never been on before we decided on a whim to drive down a dead end road and up a private lane to a house for sale. The house wasn't what we were seeking, but there was a small sign at the end of the lane that said "land for sale." Something nudged both of us to drive onto the ten acres of weeds to the north end. Something nudged us to get out and walk into the woods where we came upon a drop off to a creek and more virgin woods. It was the most serene spot either of us had ever seen. It's where we live now and its significance in the pursuit of contentment will be discussed further at the end of this book. We have both learned to listen to nudges.

I agree that we tend to notice the improbable events in our lives. Our response to them forces us to decide if they are just that - highly unlikely coincidences - or to ask if there is something deeper. At this point there will be some who will be saying "This is just the synchronicity that Jung and others talked about." The noted psychologist Carl Jung gave a lot of thought to how one should explain events, and our pre-occurrence or instantaneous awareness of them, that appear to be chance, but have a meaningful coincidence. The nature of such events would seem to require causality, but their nature seems to not require space and time which are considered essential for causality to be in play.

Albert Einstein (who clearly understood the mathematics of probability and chance) offered perhaps the best thought on this: "Coincidence is God's way of remaining anonymous."

Such events were often described as psychic, but Jung concluded that they are not brain related and not connected to our physical senses.

Jung studied ancient Chinese thinking back to King Wen of Zhou (1100BC) and the later Tao of Lao Tzu (circa 550BC) and met multiple times with Einstein to discuss space and time. He concluded that there was an ever-existing phenomenon he named synchronicity which would supplement the triad of classical physics (space, time and causality). He said that this was no more problematic or baffling than the findings of quantum physics.

For someone like myself, trained in mathematics (focus on probability and statistics), I am always saying "what are the chances?" when confronted with things that are near zero probability and can mathematically qualify as "random." This training has also made me aware of the law of truly large numbers and Littleton's law - that with enough events the likelihood of a low probability event happening increases. This is the typical explanation of miracles by those who do not attribute them to God.

There are also those who would diagnose me with either Apophenia (seeing meaningful patterns or connections within meaningless random data or events) or suffering from confirmation bias (interpreting information in a way that confirms my preconception that there is a sovereign God). Since that would lead to discussion of schizoid delusions on my part, I won't address that further in the book.

## Praying

Prayer plays a big part in our lives. In my case I do not ask God for things or intercessions. I am aware that the Bible in multiple places says to petition God (notably Ephesians 6:18 and 1Timothy 2:1) and that God will provide what is asked (Matthew 18:19).

I personally believe that I am living God's plan for my life and that He is indeed sovereign. God knows what I want (Psalm 139: You discern my thoughts and know my words before I speak them), but more importantly I need to understand what God wants from me. The overwhelming majority of my prayers are to offer thanks for all the blessings of my life - I do this multiple times every day. I have had, and still have more blessings than I can believe are possible. My other prayers (petitions) are for guidance or wisdom when faced with a challenge or a decision - I always seem to feel a nudge on how I should go. I sometimes ask (petition) for courage or strength to face a tough time along with the wisdom to make a good choice.

When Nancy was deathly ill, I prayed for guidance for us to make the right decisions in dealing with it. After she died, I sought comfort in thanking God for having given us 33 wonderful years together and two wonderful children. I asked for strength in dealing with my grief and guidance for where to go next. As I fell in love with Jeri I prayed for guidance and wisdom in rebuilding my life and guiding two more young adults who would become my step-sons.

In praying for wisdom I ask to understand my purpose and to fulfill it. Remember William Barclay's "...discover why." The Bible in Romans 8:28 guides these prayers

*"And we know that all things work together for good to them that love God,*
*to them who are called according to his purpose."*

The Book of Proverbs (24:13-14) compares the sweetness of honey to your physical senses to wisdom:
**"Know that wisdom is such to your soul;**
**If you find it, there will be a future**
**[filled with hope]."**

I pray for guidance to use the talents that God has given me to the maximum. In 1 Corinthians 12:4-11, the Apostle Paul relates the importance of wisely and properly using the gifts we have been given. My profession (after flying fighters) is in project management. I have asked for guidance to use this talent well and have been rewarded in being the volunteer leader of three projects in Africa (and one just starting in Ecuador) for my Rotary Club providing clean water, sanitation, health care and education.

These projects have changed the lives of children (and adults) beyond the comprehension of most Americans. (Frankly, while I can intellectually describe the changes, the change we have made is beyond my emotional comprehension.)

In offering prayers of gratitude, consider the power of expressing your gratitude for the good fortune of others. This is a far cry from the suppressed envy we often feel when we see someone else get something we wish had come our way. The power of being truly happy for others is incredible and kills a source of nagging dis-content.

There is a really great short saying that I have seen multiple times about what we gain from praying regularly. The answer is *"Nothing... but let me tell you what I lost: anger, ego, greed, depression, insecurity, and fear of death."* I don't agree with the "nothing" since prayer brings me contentment through gratitude for all God has given me and the "nudges" to make the best choice. Happiness replaces the Anger. Love of others replaces the Ego. Gratitude and Satisfaction replaces Greed. I have "known" I was going to die (3/13/1968) and felt only a calm resolve. You get the idea!

Several times so far I have mentioned "nudges" as how I perceive God answering my prayers or guiding me. Psalm 48:14 confirms that God "will be our guide" and John 10:27 assures us that "My sheep hear my voice."

1Kings 19:12 tells us that the guidance comes to us not in an earthquake or fire but in a gentle whisper or small still voice. The Bible (see Acts 16) also suggests God puts us into circumstances where we recognize the message or get the guidance. The book of Habakkuk is good reading also.

One last thought - there are multiple (over a dozen) places in the Bible where we are reminded that God is with us and looking out or fighting for us. Among the most meaningful for me, as a fighter pilot where, in formation air combat, we use phrases like "got your six" (meaning protecting someone's rear - the 6 o'clock position), are in Isaiah 52 and 58 where God is described as our "rear guard." In my language, God has my six.

## The End Result

Being content in your relationship with God means having absolutely no fear of life's end. I know that our life is eternal and is not constrained by our visit to this mortal existence. I am content in realizing that God is all about love and that the more love you give (to God, to family, to pets, to friends, to those in need) the richer your mortal life will be and the more content you will be as you depart it. There are many theologians that equate the third part of the Trinity (Father, Son, Holy Spirit) with love. The Father loved the Son and the Son loved the Father and we are admonished to LOVE GOD and LOVE ONE ANOTHER. That, to me, is how the Holy Spirit is within each of us.

I have used or quoted the word "know" multiple times in this discussion. There is a difference between believing and knowing something. I know for certain that God is sovereign and guiding my life. That is very contenting. The word "know" is used throughout the Bible -it is a single translation of two different Greek words used in Scripture. A book on the Gospel of John written by a very dear friend, Bill Yanney (a retired US Army Chaplain) pointed this out to me. Think about the difference as it relates to the solidity of your faith and how content you are in it.

# γινώσκω **and** οἶδα

The Greek words are pronounced ginosko and oida. The former means something you have actively come to realize (in your heart) while the later is your awareness of a fact. I pray you come to <u>know</u> God's sovereignty and that He <u>is</u> guiding your life. That leads to μετάνοια ("metanoia") - the change in your heart, discussed earlier. May you change and know.

There is a popular expression "Let Go. Let God." These words are nowhere in the Bible, but the message of trusting God and God's sovereignty are everywhere. It is not a prescription to ignore the values based on God's word - it has been mis-used by many false prophets. We will come back to this idea near the end of the book when we address the ability to be content in the moment.

## In A Word

Contentment in your relationship with God comes from your faith and thanksgiving for God's sovereignty and all the blessings that God has bestowed upon you. Contentment is amplified by being part of a community of believers who all work together to strengthen each other's faith and help one another live the life we should. Importantly, contentment entails a passion for continually learning and maturing in your relationship; being content is a continuous and on-going process. If you think "OK, I've got it" - you haven't!

# Chapter Three

## Your Life To Date
## Time For Retrospection

If you are a non-believer or a non-religious person you have probably skipped to this point in the book. This chapter and those that follow will touch on some of the same subjects again in the belief that the Bible gives us many universal truths that should be guiding the lives we live. I hope that the discussion here will cause those readers who skipped or skimmed the preceding chapter to go back for a deeper look.

I think there is one place in Chapter 2 that bears repeating here as we talk about contentment in our earthly life.

> The Bible (Luke 12:21) makes it clear that it is a matter of priorities and not a command to eschew earthly wealth.
>
> *"Yes, a person is a fool to store up earthly wealth but not have a rich relationship with God."*
>
> What does this say? Read it again. It does not say you are a fool to store up earthly wealth! It says that doing so without the relationship with God is foolish. This is why this book says contentment in your relationship with God is paramount and why it goes on in future chapters to talk about contentment in your earthly life. Surely, you can and should do both.

There is a 1942 essay written by C.S. Lewis entitled "First and Second Things." In a 1951 letter he summarized the principle he was stating:

"Put first things first and we get second things thrown in; put second things first and we lose both the first and second things."

This and the following chapters deal with the second things; the preceding chapter dealt with the first thing. Finding contentment in your relationship with God is paramount. A major aspect of that contentment is gratitude for all the blessings of your life. The focus on your own life through retrospection and introspection will hopefully trigger even deeper gratitude and strengthen your relationship with God. That triggering should take the form of the metanoia (μετάνοια) discussed near the end of chapter two.

## Focus on Our Own Lives and Contentment

There are some who would say that to focus on our contentment with our own lives smacks of selfishness - that we should be focused on making others happy. The Bible does say that loving ones neighbor as oneself is the most important commandment for our lives. We will come back later in this section to the contentment that comes from making the ones we love happy and content, but for now we need to recognize that the same Bible tells us that our own interests are important. This is best summarized in **Philippians 2:3**:

> *"Do nothing from rivalry or conceit, but in humility count others as more significant than yourselves. Let each of you look not only to his own interests, but also to the interests of others."*

Read that again carefully. It does not say that our only focus should be on the interests of others; it says our focus should be on both our own interests **and** those of others.

## The Life We Have Lived (If it all ends today)

Maybe the best reflection on this question is found in Henry David Thoreau's <u>Walden,</u> written in 1854.

*"I went to the woods because I wished to live deliberately,*
*to front only the essential facts of life,*
*and see if I could not learn what it had to teach,*
*and not,*
*when I came to die, discover that I had not lived."*

Borrowing from Walden - we should not come to the end of our life and discover that we never really lived. We should feel that, if there are a few regrets for what we didn't do, we can look at the totality of our life and be fully grateful for all the blessings we have received. Recapping from Chapter 2 (contentment with our relationship with God), we see the good that has come from even the low points in our lives. (If you skipped the preceding chapter, please go back and read about the nadirs of our lives and the importance of reflecting on them.)

The author Jonathan Swift, writing <u>Polite Conversation</u> in 1738 offered the following:
*"May you live all the days of your life."*

Or put another way (and possibly attributed to George Carlin) you should arrive at the grave shouting "...man, what a ride!"

When you look backwards can you say you have really lived all your days so far? Can you say that you wanted everything you got even though you may not have gotten everything you wanted. Can you say that you are not distressed thinking of the things you wanted and didn't get. If you can say this, it is likely that you have not repeatedly reset material wants higher and higher as soon as you started to feel satisfied (that is, content with what you have). Most people do tend to reset their wants.

## Your Destination in Retrospect

Think back to your teen or early twenty years. Where did you want to go in life? What aspirations did you have? What plans did you make? I have always loved the following saying (which was written in 1957 by cartoonist Allen Saunders and immortalized by John Lennon in 1980 in "Beautiful Boy"):

> *"Life is what happens to us
> while we are busy making other plans"*

Most have not heard the next sentence in Saunders' Reader's Digest article, but it makes a point important to us here:

> *"The trouble is most of us don't realize this
> except in retrospect
> and then life has already happened."*

STOP - think about this for a few moments. Maybe even jot down a few notes about where you wanted to go in life.

NOW - did things go the way you had envisioned? Most of us would say "somewhat." Few would say "Yes, exactly!" Even fewer would say "Not in the least"

and

NOW - can you say that you found some happiness regardless? I hope so!

In my case, at age 14 I loved science and knew that I wanted to be a research physicist specializing in high energy particle physics and teach at the college level.

At age 19, I discovered flying and my life turned upside down (literally) - they would pay me to fly airplanes and I decided to become a fighter pilot.

I also knew that I wanted a life of excitement and adventure before I settled down and raised a family. And what happened?
I flew airplanes (yes they did pay me to fly 500 mph at tree top level), managed fighter aircraft development and support projects and retired to a second career. In that next phase of my life I ended up involved in science and technology and received over 15 patents upon which companies were established and prospered.

In my third career, I trained adults to become effective project managers and team leaders, able to plan and execute projects to technical, cost and schedule objectives using effective risk management. In the meantime I launched four kids into the world as independent adults who are now married and raising kids of their own. I have loved everything I have done in a life that didn't take the path I had originally planned. Life did veer back to that path of science/technology and teaching - just not the subject I originally planned.

There is another part of that life journey that I think of often in retrospect. The life nadir at age 10 (chapter two) and the subsequent teen years influenced my thoughts about what material success meant.

As a senior in high school, applying for college, I first really became aware of our family finances. My college applications reflected an annual family (my mom and me) income of $3000 (way below the poverty level). I envisioned that phenomenal financial success would be to have a net worth of $10,000 and be making $10,000 a year. What is critical to understand here is that I never again in my life reset a financial goal, even long after I had gone many times beyond that original goal. Doing stuff I loved doing (work and family) was more important for the remainder of my working (and retired) life.

I think this single thing is an essential part of my having found contentment in life. As explained earlier in the book, this beginning set me on a path of gratefulness built upon satisfaction with what I had.

Remember in Chapter One where we quoted Socrates and Epictetus - having few wants as the key to contentment. The Biblical Greek: sufficient for yourself.

If you are not where you planned to be early in your life, the key question is whether having arrived at that destination would make you content today. We will explore the nature of your journey from this point forward later in the book. That exploration will ask if the original destination is still where you want to go and offer some ideas on figuring how to arrive at the destination this book recommends- contentment.

# Pride

The next part of the retrospective on your life to date is how you feel about the journey so far. Are you proud of what you've done and what you've accomplished? Recall that in chapter 2 we discussed pride as a sin and concluded that the sin is not giving God credit. Ecclesiastes 3:13 tells us that a sense of accomplishment or satisfaction with what we've done is one of God's gifts to us. Chapter 1 pointed out that satisfaction is at the heart of contentment. Most of us have done a few things in our lives about which we would rather forget - so this doesn't mean you have to be proud of everything. Can you create a list of actions or accomplishments about which you are proud? I recommend a list of about ten, and when complete, placed in priority order from "most proud."

STOP - write down the list and put the items in order.

I am guessing, but I am betting that your list does not include elements of material success. Guessing again, I am betting that the items on the list involve the differences you made in yourself and the world. You are right to be proud of having faced challenges and difficult tasks and having triumphed. It might be educational achievement. It might be overcoming something. It might be a recognition you received for some accomplishment. It might be a difference you made in someone else's life or in your community.

Consider the following potential hierarchy of recognition you got or wanted for something you've done and where you fit (how important was recognition?):

    0. Anonymous - I know and that's enough
    1. Acknowledgement - someone noticed/mentioned it
    2. Appreciation - someone said thanks
    3. Lauding/Honoring - you were praised
    4. Rewarded - you got something tangible
    5. Revered - you are used as the good example

Why is this exercise important? If these are the things you are most proud of in your life, what are the implications for what the rest of your life's journey should look like? Do you feel more content just thinking about all the things that made you proud? My guess is yes! Was recognition really important?

In my own life's journey I think of things in each category. I am proud of the achievement of becoming a fighter pilot (I am not a natural born pilot. As an instructor I have encountered some who are) and having served my nation in the military. I am proud of the civic action work I did in VietNam (supporting a school, orphanage and leper colony) helping kids. I am proud of the work I have done through my Rotary Club helping kids and entire villages in Africa and now Ecuador (high in the Andes). I am proud of having spent 20 years as a Boy Scout leader influencing the values and ethics of young people. I am proud of the adults my kids have become. I am proud of having tried to help those who are dealing with the loss of a spouse. I am proud of having written some children's books advocating for the adoption of rescue shelter dogs and donating all the royalties to a rescue shelter. I notice, and I hope you notice too, that each of my proudest moments involve serving. (By the way, the motto of Rotary is "Service Above Self." There is a message there that is central to finding contentment.

In the preceding paragraph I mentioned my pride in influencing the values of others. In an earlier chapter I mentioned my reaction to seeing my fundamental values violated. It is worth your time to think about what your tightly held values are and the extent to which your life has been consistent with them. We shall explore the underlying values we have at work as we make choices or decisions in a few more pages.

At this point, I recommend a five minute exercise. Assume you die six minutes from now - what are the main points you want made in your obituary. My guess is that those points will be the really important parts of your life about which you are most proud and the values you held dear. You only have five minutes to get them written down so they need to be the top of the list.

## <u>Regrets</u>

This subject obviously cuts two different ways. I suspect there are things you've done that you regret (often violating values you knew to be important) and I am almost certain there are opportunities that you regret not seizing.

Important! Do not bother dwelling on the things you regret doing. They are done, in the past, and their only value is the learning they provide for future actions.

Thinking about the things you didn't do is much more instructive and useful. What opportunities presented themselves where you didn't recognize the value at the time? What had happened that causes you to reflect on why it was a missed opportunity? Where are you thinking, "If only I had....?"

STOP - jot down a list of the missed opportunities. You are still alive, so some of them may be only "missed so far." We will come back to the subject of opportunities later in the book when we discuss serendipity.

Whoa.... what does serendipity have to do with this, you ask? Just to tweak your thought process as you read on, let me offer this. Most people haven't given much thought to serendipity - a great number have heard the word and think they know what it means. Serendipity is, on the surface, encountering something of value by accident. It is really a lot more than accidental. For now, think about things that have happened in your life that appeared to be beneficial accidents. It is an incredibly valuable concept. More on this in a later chapter.

## Blessings and Talents

As you think about your life in retrospect, consider all the blessings you have been given and how you used them to the best of your ability. Blessings are gifts we are given as human beings - very often they are a talent for doing a specific thing. Too broad a request? Consider the following:

- Have you had good health? How did you take advantage of this?
- Are you possessed of physical attributes like strength, agility, or dexterity?
- Are you creative? Can you produce music or art?
- Are you a thinker? Can you figure stuff out? Can you apply logic?
- Were you born in a society where you could fully use your talents?

An important part of taking a retrospective look at our lives is to ask the question of whether we have taken full advantage of the blessings and talents we have been given as an individual human being.

Think about those blessings and talents where you can answer a resounding YES. Yes, I have fully developed and used the gifts I have been given. Has the use of these helped bring you contentment? My guess is yes.

Now think about those areas where you didn't get your "fair share" of a particular talent and satisfactorily pursued something requiring that gift. Are you more proud of that accomplishment than places where you are naturally talented? (See prior discussion on pride as a reminder).

Now think of gifts or talents you have where you really didn't use it to the fullest. Do these form any part of your pattern of regrets? (See prior discussion on regrets as a reminder)

In my own life, recall (Chapter two, nadir #1) that I was an un-athletic, clumsy kid who discovered a passion for flying airplanes, especially ones that fly very fast and fly in formation with other airplanes. I didn't get my "fair share" of coordination (I never did learn to roller or ice skate for example and took forever learning to ride a bike) and hence becoming a fighter pilot is first on my "proud of" list presented earlier.

I have a natural talent for organizing things like projects and for teaching - I am proud of having used those gifts to their fullest. I have close to zero musical talent (I love listening), but I own a keyboard and a guitar and have tried, I really have.
I like to delude myself that I have a talent for expressing myself in writing and hence am engaged here in creating a second "serious" book after two children's books. (OK, not as serious as dealing with the death of your spouse). If I didn't get my fair share of writing talent, then I am doing my best to make up for that shortfall.

We will come back to this subject later, but it is useful to think here about what your gifts are and to assess, in retrospect, your success in using them to the fullest.

## Choices and Decisions

Your entire life has been a never-ending series of choices and decisions. Without thinking a lot about this fact, you undoubtedly realize that they fall into several categories: inconsequential ones that made little or no difference after you made them, important ones that you stuck with, important ones that you later modified, and important ones that you wanted to change and couldn't. You also realize, in retrospect, that your life to this date has followed a path determined by those choices. Let's put those choices and decisions into general areas:

- Ones where you see the benefit of having made the decision you did for how your life has played out so far. Consider especially the ones where you later decided to change direction. Ask yourself what criteria you considered at the time in making or changing your choice.

- Ones that you regret making, especially those where you couldn't redirect your pathway or, if you could, where the detour that decision produced had a lasting impact. Again ask yourself what criteria you considered in making that choice. If you were able to change direction later, ask yourself what was wrong with the criteria used in the initial decision.

STOP - take a few minutes and think about the consequential choices you have made and your decision criteria. Maybe jot down a few notes as reminders as you reminisce. Consider at least the following life areas:

- Your relationship with God
    Your decision to believe in God and to be a
    person of faith is indeed one of life's major
    decisions. How did you make that decision?
- Your relationship with people important to you
- Your choice of close friends
- Your attitude and effort with respect to education
- Your career or skill development choices
- Your choice of a significant other
- Your decisions on how to allocate the time you have each day or week.
- Your behavioral choices, to include your reaction to obstacles or roadblocks
- Have there been opportunities that just "popped up?" What did you choose?

What we are looking for here is a learning experience where you really and seriously evaluate the impact of choices on the life lived to date. If you believe you have been the victim of bad circumstances, this is the time for you to seriously think about your reaction to those circumstances. We will come back to this in Chapter Five.

I have spent a lot of time analyzing my own life choices in an attempt to improve the decisions I make in the future. Here is a smattering of things I have thought about.

In the years after my dad abandoned our family placing us in serious financial straits, I remember thinking about how I needed to excel in high school so I could get into and afford college if I wanted to pursue the sciences. I would not become a victim of my circumstances. I remember thinking in my teens and twenties how I wanted to avoid marrying young so I could first get on a firm footing and never be eaten up later in life by what adventures I may have missed. I avoided serious girlfriend relationships - one might become serious.

In USAF pilot training I saw others partying hard and decided if I were to get the assignment I wanted, there wasn't time for (much of) that.

In choosing a career after the Air Force I vividly remember placing the enjoyment of the job above the pay. I had four job offers following interviews and chose the one that sounded like the most fun; it was also the lowest pay of the four. Had I not made that decision I wouldn't have returned to science and technology and become a named inventor.

I do think often about other decisions (including some "pop-up" opportunities) and where my life might have gone had I chosen differently and conclude in each case I am happy with the decision I made. An example of one of those was when the Air Force was looking for fighter pilots to send to Med School to become pilot/doctors. My life certainly would have been different from today, but I don't regret the decision to say no. Others involve applying for The Thunderbirds air-show team and Test Pilot School - I did both and was selected for neither, but had I not applied I would always wonder.

Making decisions presupposes that you have some set of decision criteria upon which they are based. These are usually the values you hold dear and which guide your life. For most of us those values tend to be Biblically based: 1 Corinthians 2:16 talks of thinking in Godly ways, Romans 8:5-6 talks of being fully in the spirit of God, Ephesians 2:10 talks of us being created to do good works. Recall that John Adams said that the US Constitution was made for a moral and religious people and inadequate for those who did not hold to these values.

There is a particularly good book, written in 1944 by C.S. Lewis (The Abolition of Man) that speaks very pointedly about the values that define our humanity and existence of those who wish to kill those values or rules that guide our society. He makes the point that those who wish us to ignore these "rules" are often seeking power over us and call such rules sentimental, old-fashioned religious sanctions, or inherited taboos. He warns against those who want to influence young minds (he refers to them as "intellectuals") to question and reject these. He specifically makes the point that values are what society uses to constrain instincts. He cites sexual desire as instinctually seeking gratification while traditional values and morals place constraint on that gratification. He further states that we have no instinctual urge to keep promises.

Lewis provides several pages of such traditional values drawing, not just from the Bible, but from many other sources. Among those critically important values (beyond the direct proscriptions and prescriptions in the Bible) Lewis includes:

- Not bringing misery to one's fellow man (cruelty)
- Not uttering words that wound
- Speaking kindness and showing good will
- Not being unconcerned with others' misfortune
- Honoring and having reverence for one's native land
- Providing for one's self and members of one's house
- Respecting the dead
- Loving and nurturing one's offspring
- Drawing false boundaries or speaking falsehoods
- Respecting both common and private property
- Not being bribed
- Men not striking a woman
- Not being a coward (better to die than live in shame)
- Loving learning

Let me take a moment here to expound on the "honor and reverence for one's country" cited by C.S. Lewis. There is a Teddy Roosevelt comment embraced by Eleanor Roosevelt about being a good citizen that is particularly important in an age where only one percent of the population serves in the military or as a first responder. Read this and then stop and ponder for a moment, "Am I a citizen worthy of having someone fight and die for me?" Borrowing the words of JFK - what do I do FOR my country. This is an important value!

The word "values" is used dozens of times in this book. The subject of "values" has an interesting development in the Bible. There are three different Greek words (ἰσόψυχος, λογισμός, and φιλοτιμέομαι) that carry the idea and describe different dimensions. They are used a total of only six times in the New Testament. Without turning this section into a Greek lesson here are the main ideas conveyed: being like-minded, having the same outlook and being similarly motivated as others on a moral issue (Phil 2:20); having affection for what is personally honored or aspiring/devoting oneself to something honorable via ambition (Rom15:20, 2Cor5:9, and 1Thes4:11); and reaching a personal opinion or thought through logical reasoning (Rom2:15 and 2Cor10:4). What is most instructive here is that the same author uses different words in the same book to assure the intended meaning is conveyed. Truly understanding one's own values and living one's life in accordance with them is not a simple thing.

The 2017 book <u>Dying on Purpose</u> has an appendix where the author lists 419 possible values which may provide the foundation for your purpose in life. Contentment and gratitude are among them (of course). As an aside, the author was inspired to write the book by a near death experience.

I hope that as you conclude this retrospective part of this book, you have truly taken the time to think about the things you are proud of, the things you regret, the values that you hold dear in your decision-making, and the outcomes of the specific choices you have made along with the criteria that led to either a good or less good outcome. Understanding these things will be of value to you.

## Happiness From Having "Stuff"

Some would say it is hedonistic (and hence automatically bad or evil) to focus on the happiness derived from having material possessions - stuff. Stop for a moment and think of something you own that brings you pleasure. Got it in your thoughts?

OK - now ask WHY it brings you happiness.

Now ask - "Does it contribute to my CONTENTMENT?"

My guess is that you will see the distinction - short term enjoyment of it (like driving a sports car or playing golf with top quality clubs) versus soul satisfying contentment.

In my own personal experience, I find contentment in owning original antique art (to include antique schoolgirl needlework samplers). It has nothing to do with the monetary value. The contentment comes from marveling in the God-given creative talent of the person who produced it. I am grateful for the opportunity to be the current owner enjoying their creation and in the passing it on to someone else to enjoy after I am gone. See the difference? In some ways this comes back to lessons of Chapter Two - I am content in a beautiful world God created including the creativity with which he blessed the makers of these material things.

There is an entire book I recently discovered on this subject: The Things of Earth by Joe Rigney. I strongly recommend it. He makes the point that sin is not inherent in "stuff" - it is how we view "stuff" in our hearts. 1 Timothy 4:3-5 captures the thought - "everything created by God is good, nothing is to be rejected if it is received with thanksgiving." Enjoying "stuff" celebrating its creator and being thankful should not result in feelings of guilt. Praise and thanksgiving increases the enjoyment. I have a few more words in Chapter Seven about mortal "stuff."

## In A Word

Our retrospective look should have led you to understand how your life is different from what you planned or intended and why (discovery of your talents, the reasons for and the results of your choices and decisions). You should understand what has made you proud and what regrets you carry with you as a burden. Hopefully you have had a chance to think more deeply about the values you hold dear and which have motivated your actions. You should understand what it is in your life that brings you contentment.

# Chapter 4:
# Your Life Today
# Time For Introspection

In the prior chapter, you were asked to think about how you got to where you are today and to reflect on the ups and downs of the journey you've trod so far.

## Are You Content With Where You Are Today?

This is the obvious big question for this chapter. If you can answer a resounding YES to this question, then skim past the rest of this chapter and the next and focus on Chapter 6.

If you wish you were happier with where you are, then this and next chapter will offer some insights for getting there.

Topics for this chapter include:
- What makes you happy on a day-to-day and week-to-week basis?
- How often do you feel dis-content and why?
- How often are you angry and why?
- Are the things you do in living the things you'd really like to be doing?
- What motivates you and do your motivations vary?

### Real Time Happiness?

Ask yourself what percentage of your time each day, or each week, is spent truly happy and content. When are you happy or content? What things do you most look forward to in your day-to-day life? What things that you do always seem to be over too soon?

Really - stop and jot down some notes since putting your thoughts on paper forces you to better define what those times are. After listing these things, rank order them. Consider at least the following:

-Your work life
-Your leisure activities and amusements
-Your family life and relationships
-Your adventures (things you need to plan for, then do)
-Special occasions
-Your service to others
-Your time devoted to God (including being grateful for blessings)

Do you see any common threads among what's on your list?

What are they?
Which one of these best captures the true focus of your life?

In our book <u>Thanks For The Dance</u> we offer an exercise to list, in priority order, the dozen happiest moments of your life. The intent of this exercise is to lead the reader in seeing the role of your late spouse in those moments.

You might take a moment and try that right now, starting with the list you just prepared. Once done, which of the above categories do most of the dozen fall into? It is not uncommon for a large number to involve those you love - there is a very important message there.

For me, number one on the list was (and still is) becoming a parent - the transition from adult to parent, it only happens once in your life. There are really two types of stimuli that produce happiness - those of the senses and those of the mind. Our senses hear wonderful sounds, our eyes see amazing sights, we taste fabulous food and we tend to feel happy.

This is fine unless we evolve to what might be defined as hedonism - sensual pleasure is the ultimate good. As a contrast, the philosopher Aristotle evolved the concept of eudaimonia - the mental happiness that comes from finding purpose and meaning. Modern researchers in wellness or well being suggest there are three contributors - hedonic (sensual), eudaimonic (mental), and relaxation (a combination of both). So listen to the music and the sounds of nature that you love, figure out how to live a life filled with purpose and meaning (hint - loving others and making the ones you love happy is a great start followed by making full use of your God-given talents), and being able to relax (physically and mentally).

The idea of finding purpose in life appears in almost all cultures. The Japanese have a word for it:

# Ikigai　生き甲斐

The literal translation is knowing your reason for being, the thing you live for. It usually refers to the source of value in one's life or the things that make one's life worthwhile.

Two other terms in Japanese culture that parallel the concept of IKIGAI are:

# Kenshō 見性　and　Satori 悟り

which refer to coming to understand ones true nature. Teachers point out that coming to this understanding is a multi-faceted process: growth through overcoming challenges and growth via insight (often while searching for that true nature and the reason for being.) This is what retrospection and introspection are all about.

The use if the word "hedonism" suggests all sorts of negative moral connotations so it is fun to me that renowned pastor John Piper devised the phrase "Christian Hedonism." I suspect that was designed to make people do a double take as I did the first time I heard it in 2018. Piper summarizes the philosophy as "God is most glorified in us when we are most satisfied in Him." The thoughts parallel those in this book and while Piper doesn't link being satisfied with contentment as I do here, he points out that we seek happiness with the manifestations of God's creation and glorify God when we offer thanks and praise for God's blessings and the enjoyment of His creation.

Piper explains that he chose to use the term hedonism to differentiate between our happiness being the highest good (classical hedonism) and that by pursuing the highest good will result in our greatest happiness (Christian Hedonism). This is consistent with what this book put forth in Chapter Two. Being satisfied with our blessings and expressing gratitude for them is the core ingredient of contentment.

Cicero, in about 50BC explained that

**"Gratitude is not only the greatest of virtues,**

**but the parent of all the others."**

There is a really popular saying that no one found themselves on their deathbed saying "I wish I'd spent more time at the office." Another is that "there is always time to make money, but the opportunity to build treasured memories is rarer."

That does not mean that your work life can't be a major source of your happiness. For some it is.

For many, the greatest happiness comes from taking part in what one would call adventures. Adventures are more than climbing mountains, white water rafting, flying aerobatics in an open cockpit biplane, on safari in Africa, visiting an exotic place, or doing something with an element of risk. I have done all those things and I can be easily categorized as an adventure seeker or risk taker. Having done them, I will never look back someday and say, "I wish I had..." I have been doing them while I can. One of my guiding sayings is from Helen Keller:

## *"Life is Either An Adventure, or Nothing!"*

I have been blessed to live a life where almost everything I do is something I look forward to and which seems to be over too soon. For the better part of my life flying airplanes was near the top of the list - I always looked forward to it and the time to land always seemed to come too quickly. I cannot tell you how many times I thought to myself "...and they are paying me money to do this." Adventures with those I love ranks high on the list (from Boy Scout backpacking with my son to helping AIDS orphans in Africa's most dangerous slum accompanied by my wife) and I am still planning adventures.

While writing this book I took time out for a couple of adventures I had been hoping to have for many decades: standing atop the Great Wall of China, visiting Tibet, and mingling with the world's population of Quokkas on Rottnest Island. Putting together a three to five day leadership and project management training class and then engaging students in places as diverse as New York City and the grand canyon (the National Park Service Training Center is there) always went too fast.

Before you read on, please close the book and take the time to think about these things, as we will come back to this subject in the next chapter.

# There Are Potholes

So... about this time you are thinking how all this doesn't sound like the reality of life. It is all unicorns happily dancing under the rainbows. As the Saunders quote mentioned earlier says - life happens and the road of life's journey does have potholes. As we said in chapter 6 of <u>Thanks For The Dance</u> just when you think you are getting back on a smooth path after losing your spouse, you encounter the potholes. What we offer there is that the key to handling the potholes is expecting them and figuring out how to respond to them. We reiterate that advice here.

Identifying the potholes: If your destination in life is contentment (and the fact that you've read this far in a book that promotes that view suggests you are buying into that philosophy) then the obvious pothole is dis-content. What causes you to feel discontentment? Again, we ask that you stop for a moment and jot down the things that lead you feel discontent. Consider at least the following ten general categories:

    1. The circumstances you find yourself in (financial, relationships, stressful)

    2. The injustices you see or experience (personal to world-wide)

    3. Disappointment that things didn't go the way you wanted

    4. Resentment of things that have happened or things people have done to you and Bitterness over unfairness (or what you see as bad luck)

    5. Impatience that things aren't happening at the pace you want

    6. Envy or jealousy that others have more, seem happier, or have "better" lives

    7. Anger over any number of things

8. Worry (or anxiety) about any number of things
9. Loneliness
10. Conflict with others

Just a quick check - there are ten categories above and the math is easy. What percent of them can you say apply to you. I feel as though I have found contentment in life and I couldn't say zero percent so I suspect at least some of these resonated with you.

Reacting to the potholes"

The objective here is to understand why you aren't more content. All of these represent your decision on how to react to something - and make no mistake it is a decision you make, even if subconsciously.

In The Book of Joy the Dali Lama suggests building mental immunity to negative emotions (reactions to events), which therefore limits the role of fear and anger and the stress they produce. He offers that negative reactions make it harder to place events into perspective such as the 25 year retrospective discussed in Chapter Two of this book. Negative reactions tend to be judgments and criticisms rather than analyzing the opportunities inherent in the situation; he strongly recommends what he calls "analytic meditation" aimed at lengthening the reaction time between stimulus and response. When you find your gut reaction being worry, frustration, anger or sadness it is time to reconsider the response. Will worrying help? Will frustration bring you anything but stress? Will anger benefit anyone? Is one's reaction to sadness best found in seeking pity or seeking comfort from another (remember the old adage that sharing the burden of bad times makes them only half as bad).

Practicing "analytic meditation" is totally consistent with the admonitions in the Bible (Proverbs) to be "slow to speak." For the Christian the obvious reaction to negative events in our lives is to turn to God and His word in prayer - this is the delayed reaction that is advocated here.

Think about situations where you feel you need to be apologetic and react to your perceived "transgression" with "I'm sorry for ..." There is a much more positive way to handle those situations and it involves our old friend gratitude. Suppose you are late for a meeting - do you apologize for being late or do you couch your acknowledgment of being late in another way, such as "Thanks for waiting for me." Think of all the situations where you feel the need to apologize and where an apology is appropriate. Is there a way of showing gratitude for the understanding of the other person?

Think about how you react when someone says something with which you disagree.

You can react by an immediate rebuttal (attack and place them on the defensive), with a more conciliatory "Yes, but..." before launching into the rebuttal, or thirdly with a "Yes, and..." where you expand the discussion to include other points of view. Even when you totally disagree with what someone has said, the discussion will go a lot further and be more civil if you ask them to explain their position further with a simple question such as "how did you arrive at that conclusion?" or "how do you know that's true?" Have dialogue, not debate!

Your life will be a lot more content if you handle potential conflicts in this manner, rather than mounting challenges directly. There is a big difference between reacting (quickly at the gut level) and responding (after thoughtful consideration or prayer) non-confrontationally seeking dialogue. Offering a thoughtful measured response has two advantages:

· It allows you to hear more about the other person's perspective and maybe hear something you didn't know and

· It keeps the discussion civil while giving you the opportunity to insert your objections in the form of questions, rather than direct challenges.

Even at the least, reacting in this manner:

· Gains you a better understanding of why someone feels differently than you do about an issue,

· May give the other person pause to reconsider their position (if they don't have good answers for your questions) and

· Preserves the relationship with that person. Those six words are worth thinking about - when you negotiate something with someone the goal is two-fold: to come up with a result you can both live with and to preserve the relationship.

## Nine Potholes

With respect to the list of ten paths toward discontent above - if you think back to Chapter Two you will recognize some of these from our discussion of your relationship with God. A cross section of Biblical wisdom and advice was offered there and some of it bears repeating here.

Circumstances: The Biblical admonition to be grateful in all circumstances is certainly much easier to say than it is to embrace. The central theme of our prior book, Thanks For The Dance, is captured in its subtitle - Transforming Grief Into Gratitude When Your Spouse Dies. The loss of a spouse is among life's worst circumstances. It is hard to be content when you are being crushed with grief. It's harder when the loss brings with it other challenges such as financial problems. Make no mistake there is nothing, no magical formula that will take away the pain of such loss.

Are you truly grateful in all circumstances? Do you feel like you don't have much to be thankful for? Think about your personal circumstances. If there is one thing that spending the last decade leading Rotary projects in Africa has shown me, it is that anyone reading this book has a lot to be grateful for. They should be truly thankful in their current circumstances.

Ponder for a moment:

· You turn on the faucet and out comes clean drinkable water. All of our projects have involved providing safe water to people for whom water is a scarce resource, where often they walk miles to obtain water from a polluted stream. We have dug boreholes and provided rainwater harvest and solar powered chlorination through our projects.

· You turn on another faucet and out comes warm water for washing up. One of our projects involved solar water heating and another provided training in proper hand washing - something not routine when water is a scarce commodity.

· You flip the switch and lights come one. All of our projects have involved providing electricity using solar or wind energy. That electricity not only provided lighting, but also ran the borehole pumps providing clean safe water.

· You relieve yourself in a bathroom and flush a toilet. Several of our projects have provided the first sanitation beyond an open pit latrine or a shallow trench down the middle of a dirt path between shacks. Two and a half **billion** people in the world do not have access to a toilet.

· You are sick or injured and have a doctor or emergency room available. Two of our projects have provided a clinic where there was none before.

So - embrace the first pillar in the Dali Lama's prescription for joy - put everything in perspective. You do have a lot to be grateful for! For the Christian this perspective is gratitude to God for the blessings He has given you. You can, indeed, be grateful "in all circumstances.

Oh, and by the way, in years of working with those living in what we would call dire circumstances, I have an observation. I have found African slum dwellers to be more grateful for what they DO HAVE than many Americans I encounter.

These people do not ignore or deny all the negatives (like drunk, AIDS infected men who believe they can cure their AIDS by raping a virgin of any age or the odor of open ditch sewers outside their shack); they are grateful for the positives.

In their own personal deprivation, they seem willing to share and help others.

I think often of two different men I have encountered in the slums who inspire me.

· the first lost everything he had when he fled the slum with his wife and daughter ahead of machete-wielding youth upset at election results that favored someone of his same tribal background. He was grateful for having escaped.

· the second made it to the organization with which we worked as a youngster, crippled with polio and abandoned by his parents, by pulling himself through the open sewers with his forearms to the center. The workers there got him surgery so he can now walk with crutches and offered education. Long story short. While I was there on one of my project visits he graduated from college (think about that for a minute!) and showed his gratitude by coming back to the project as a teacher to help others. This "pay it forward" attitude is not uncommon.

Injustices:   We experience or see things that just don't seem fair. Do such things consume you or do they act as a catalyst to do something about them? Do we see things happen to others that seemed undeserved?

These things happen - it is up to us to figure out how to respond when we see what we categorize as unjust.

Part of that response is how we explain injustices. Do we frequently see the injustice as perpetrated upon us, making us the victim? It is easier to think of ourselves as the victim since that absolves us from having to take any action or change anything in many cases.

If you see yourself as the victim of unjust circumstances or action by others, do you get angry and strike back or do you figure out what needs to change so you are not the victim in the future? A part of the "figuring out" may lead to the discovery that your choices played a part and that changing what you do may prevent a recurrence.

It was not my fault that my dad abandoned us when I was ten and dropped my mom and me into relative poverty. I never thought of myself as a victim, but rather set up a course of action to deal with it. Working among the truly impoverished in Africa's slums I found that a feeling of victim-hood was rare. It was the circumstance they found themselves in, they were grateful for what they did have, and they were determined to advance their circumstances through personal effort.

Disappointment:   We all want certain things to happen, we want to feel happiness, and we want people to do certain things. Not everything goes according to our plan. Remember from Chapter Three - life is what happens while you are busy planning. There will be times when you feel disappointment - that is part of being human. It is impossible to be content when disappointed. The key is how much of your life is consumed thinking about what didn't happen - this is where you can refocus on the good that did happen and constructively think about how to make the thing you want a reality.

Resentment and Bitterness:  These are subtly different.

        First, Resentment -  When we see others getting what *we want* our disappointment at not getting it takes a further step.

The Dali Lama points to the thousand year old Tibetan Buddhist technique of "Lojong" to lessen one's self absorption in getting what you want; he stresses that training your mind to avoid obsessing over what you want and the resulting disappointment. Such obsessing will never result in greater overall happiness.

The overall thrust of Lojong is to provide a set of antidotes to the mental habits that cause suffering. The teachings describe craving as one the three main poisons we embrace. Meditating on what provokes resentment itself is among the elements of Lojong training. You don't have to practice Buddhism to see the wisdom in this teaching. The Bible is quite clear on the importance of not obsessing on getting the things of this mortal world - again the Buddhists and the Christians embrace the same universal truths.

Second, Bitterness - It is common to think of bitterness and resentment as the same thing. The reason it is listed separately here is to flag the anger one feels at being treated unfairly. We may resent what someone has done to us and this offense leads to anger towards the offender. This is the reason it is separate here - bitterness is generally directed at someone for something they have done and grows stronger in our heart the more we think about it. The feeling can escalate into spitefulness toward the offender.

It is impossible to be truly content when you are trapped in a past filled with bitterness. Regardless of how much you wish for a different past, it is what it is. The reason we hold onto bitterness, the anger it precipitates and the debilitating impact it has on our happiness and contentment is simple - we are unable to forgive the person for the offense.

Most religious teachings stress the importance of forgiveness - In Christianity Romans 12:18 says "If it is possible, as far as it depends on you, live at peace with everyone" while Ephesians 4:32 says to forgive each other.

Nobel prize winner Desmond Tutu points out that not forgiving keeps us tethered to the one who harmed us and that person becomes our jailer- holding the keys to our happiness. If you truly believe that you have been so seriously wronged that forgiveness is impossible you need to read Tutu's book <u>The Book of Forgiving.</u> In it, he tells of the families of those tortured and murdered during the struggles against South African apartheid and how they found forgiveness as the only path toward reconciliation and future peace. It is a powerful book.

Martin Luther King, Jr. offered a very powerful observation:

*"We must develop and maintain the capacity to forgive. He who is devoid of the power to forgive is devoid of the power to love."*

<u>Impatience:</u>    When you have an expectation that something will be done within a certain timeframe it is easy to feel impatience. We all find ourselves impatient from time to time. Our early discussion about visiting the DMV is the classic case (and the source for laugh-out-loud humor in a film like Zootopia where the DMV workers are sloths). I already mentioned the experience of driving along a narrow British country road and coming upon a flock of sheep moving at their own pace.

You chose to let impatience escalate to discontent and even anger at being delayed. Impatience can of course be even longer term - taking a long time to get a promotion you want or waiting for a contractor to finish work on a house project (again captured in humor in a film like "Money Pit" where the completion estimate is always "two weeks"). Try to find the humor in those things that make you impatient or tell yourself that is isn't worth becoming discontent.

<u>Envy/Jealousy:</u>    Think back to Chapter One and the quotes from Epictetus and Socrates. Not being content with what you have (and in fact even being grateful for what you have) is the foundation of most envy of others or jealousy that someone has more. A look at history shows that many who sought positions of tyrannical power started by sowing the seeds of discontent that others had more than those they hoped to rule. Promoting an attitude that it is "us and them" when it comes to inequality of wealth has become progressively more common starting a hundred years ago. The tyrant-to-be promises to make things fairer and more equal - history tells us this doesn't usually turn out well. People are not equal in talents and motivation - expecting equal results is illogical.

It is best to go with the tenth commandment in the Bible - not to covet anything that is your neighbor's. The words of Socrates make the point well that if you constantly want for more that you will never be happy with what you ever have.

<u>Anger:</u>    We talked a fair amount about anger in a Biblical context back in Chapter Two. What is worth repeating here is that anger is a normal part of being human and that the Bible recognizes that. What is significant from that discussion is understanding where anger can lead us - places we don't want to go if we value contentment. Repeating another important point from Chapter Two - clearly being angry is incompatible with being content.

Recall we said that there is a body of thought that considers anger as always being a secondary emotion. This means you chose to be angry because of some other emotion that is experienced first.  For example, you may be disappointed at someone - then become angry with them or embarrassed by someone - then become angry with them.

Anger can also be considered the "fight" (as opposed to "flight") response to fear. It is also common during grief - you can be upset that you experienced this loss and then try to affix blame. We suggested that you try to think of a situation where you have gone immediately to anger? There is almost always some underlying or trigger emotion. It is not unusual to be angry with your kids over something; say they come in much later than agreed. The primary emotion is worry that something has happened to them or disappointment that they failed to live up to an agreement. If you skimmed over the section on anger in Chapter Two, I recommend you go back and read it again.

Worry:   We are all predisposed to think about things that can go wrong. That is a normal part of living in a complex society and at the heart of understanding risks. There is a subtle transition from thinking about the risk of an undesirable event and even taking some action to avoid or mitigate the impact from that thing happening. (I teach for almost a day about addressing risks in managing projects - most of that is applicable to daily living as well). Where we become discontent is not in thinking about what might go wrong, but in being able to think of little else. Worry itself is not productive unless it motivates one to figure out how to address the risk. Worry itself will not help solve a problem and the mental state actually aims one away from doing something productive and effective about the source of the worry. Worry, of course, is the foundation of fear and anxiety. John Locke noted that "What worries you, masters you."

The Bible, in Matthew 6:27 offers this counsel:

> *"Can any one of you by worrying*
> *add a single hour to your life?"*

The Dali Lama agrees with this Biblical universal wisdom and often points out the futility of worrying, pointing out that if there is no way to overcome a tragedy then there is nothing gained by worrying about it, and if there is something that can be done, then there is no need for worry - do what needs to be done. Indeed, for the Christian, this Bible verse is a universal truth (recognized by a non-Christian). The Christian has a big advantage over the Dali Lama in his ability to turn to an omnipotent and omniscient God in prayer.

The year 2020 gave many a reason to worry (the dreaded COVID with a 99.8% survival rate) and react with fear of death. I have pondered "why so much fear?" Perhaps fear was greatest in those who saw this life as "all there is" with no hereafter with God. That must be scary! (My wife and I both had COVID in late 2020 and subsequently donated plasma to help others. Neither of us felt afraid. )

Do you worry about dying? The Dali Lama has a simple response to that question. The best way to approach death is with joy about what lies ahead and satisfaction with the life you've lived. (The Dali Lama and a Christian like myself have very different perspectives about that joy, but it is joy nonetheless. The Christian's joy comes from having been made right with God through Jesus Christ.) The next best way is without fear (this is a natural part of living and I am not afraid of what lies ahead). From a Christian perspective, the non-believer should be fearful because they have fallen short without the grace of God. If these don't capture your answer, he says to then at least approach death with no regrets.

For less regrets consider Harriet Beecher Stowe's observation:

> *"The bitterest tears shed over graves are for*
>
> *words left unsaid and deeds left undone."*

Think back to the quote from Thoreau's Walden in chapter three - the worst thing would be to come to the end of life and realizing you had never really lived. Most older people when asked about their regrets talk about things they didn't do as opposed to regretting things they did. The Dali Lama goes on to say that one should feel calm and peace when facing death, having savored each moment by having been fully alive. The Christian would feel that calm from God knowing what was in our heart and the strength of our faith. One's hope, trust and strength comes from having been saved. Or, on a much lighter note, for the Harry Potter fans out there, death, according to Dumbledore, is the next great adventure. So many questions will be answered - for me personally this joyous adventure will involve understanding so many things that I now accept only on faith.

I don't know how many readers have ever known they were going to die (not just afraid they were, but resolved to it as a fact), but I have.

On March 13, 1968, on a night combat mission in VietNam, I experienced exactly what the Dali Lama is saying. While I was taking action to avoid the 50 caliber ground-fire aimed at me coming off a target at 500 feet pulling 4 g's, I saw no way out and felt that sense of calm resolve (not panic or fear) that I was about to die. To paraphrase the 23rd Psalm - I have flown through the valley of the shadow of death without fear for I knew God was with me. (P.S. Flight lead spotted the source and both of us then went face-to-face with him. He lost!)

I have been asked if I was ever fearful in combat. Yes -on a night mission delivering ordnance 100' from our own guys - afraid that I would make a 100' mistake going 500mph. All survived -later extracted by helicopter. Met 3 of them in 2018.

Every day has been a bonus day since 3/13/68. I am still working on the "joy" part, but key to that, is continuing to grow in my Christian faith as well as contemplating how well I have loved others and brought them joy and happiness, the extent to which my life has mattered to others, and the extent to which I have lived my life with purpose.

Loneliness:   This subject gets a fair amount of discussion in Thanks For The Dance since loneliness is expected after the loss of one's spouse. We used the analogy of being alone in a deep hole where you only briefly see the sun each day. It was left for last here to leave you with a final thought about the role of friends and community in your journey toward contentment. Loneliness is a major cause of depression.

Remember our discussion in Chapter Two about the importance of community in the maturation of our relationship with God? For those who do not feel part of a community, and we humans are by nature social creatures, the source of discontent is less easily defined. Something is missing, but it is subtler. Keep in mind that one of the most severe punishments that is meted out to prisoners is solitary confinement - is so effective because of our need for human interaction.

Recall that King Solomon in Ecclesiastes 4:10 says that we should "pity anyone who falls and has no one to help them up." Having true friends is important. Recall that the angel Clarence in "It's A Wonderful Life" told George Bailey that "no man is a failure who has friends." More on all this later.

To test for loneliness all it takes is asking yourself how much of your happy or content time involves friends and family.

On a personal note, after my wife's death I came to realize that I was falling in love with Jeri when I was on a business trip and driving through a spectacularly beautiful part of Scotland and wished I could be sharing it with her. The contentment that comes from sharing good times with other people is the flip side of discontent caused by loneliness. Just as bad times are only half as bad when the burden is shared, good times are twice as good when shared with someone special. Francis Bacon, writing his essay Of Friendship in 1625, captured it perfectly:

*"The worst solitude is to have no real friendships."*

## The Tenth Pothole - Conflict

While the existence of conflict in our lives is such an obvious source of discontent that you might think it wastes time here to even discuss it. In reality there is an immense amount to say here. I would like to introduce what are perhaps new ways to think about conflict and to lessen its contribution to discontent.

1. **Two Dimensions:** Experts in conflict management tell us that we should look at interpersonal conflict in terms of assertiveness and cooperativeness. When someone holds beliefs or desires very strongly they tend to be very assertive with others in getting their way.
The entrance of conflict depends on those with whom they deal - if both parties feel strongly and are assertive there will be intense competition to prevail and hence conflict. The conflict can be ended by either compromise (each gives up a little and maybe harbors a little resentment - not good for being truly content as discussed earlier) or collaboration (where they figure out how both can be happy with the outcome).

When the second party doesn't hold strong beliefs, they will normally acquiesce to the assertive person.

Another possible outcome is someone who wants to avoid conflict at all costs and will disengage without any form of resolution. This works only when the avoider is not constantly reminded of the conflicting view. The other type of avoidance could be called ipsedixitism where people hold unfounded (unsupported by logical argument) opinions that they state very assertively, but are very reluctant to engage in any dialogue about the view because they are trying to force them on others. Such people could be called misologists since they want to avoid logical debate.

It is fairly common to just avoid highly assertive people, but, when one sees them rolling over others and spreading their position widely, one becomes less comfortable the more strongly the competing belief was held and believed. If you hold beliefs that others reject it is truly hard to be content when constantly encountering opposing beliefs and seeing large numbers acquiescing to something you don't believe. It is actually less stressful to engage and state your views than it is to seethe with discontent. Engaging demands that you become better prepared to state and defend your belief, unlike the misologists.

    2. **Desires Evolve:** This one might surprise you, but if you have thought about the causes of discontent in this chapter, you will see how conflict arises from a combination of factors already discussed.

Follow this logic: We all have desires - things we want - that are a normal part of being human. The desires may rest quietly in the background or become the foundation for goals. Where we get into trouble is when those desires start becoming something else - when they become demands and we feel we need to take action to satisfy them.

Now we are becoming discontent (if you are thinking "we should all have goals" don't worry we will come back to this later).

Here is where the danger starts. When we feel the need to take action to satisfy a demand they can subtly transition into needs - things we cannot do without and where action becomes essential to satisfy the need. We now become even more discontent at having unmet needs.

This evolution can even continue to the point where we set expectations that others should be meeting our needs which leads to *disappointment, resentment* or even *bitterness* that others are not meeting our needs. The final stage is when we feel enough *anger* that we need to confront or even punish those who aren't meeting the needs we expect them to meet. And there we find ourselves in serious conflict. The word "satisfy" is the key. Once a desire leads to dis-satisfaction at not having the desire fulfilled we can no longer be content. The more important a desire becomes in determining our actions, the less content we become and the more likely we are to find ourselves in conflict. Feelings of resentment that our needs are not being satisfied and anger at those who are failing to meet our needs can result in one feeling they are a victim. If one sees themselves as a victim, there must be someone who is victimizing us and we then direct our anger at the victimizer. This shows up in conflict-filled marriages and in many employment situations. Among those who believe that the government has a responsibility to meet our needs, it leads to the expectation that government will meet those needs, and resentment when government doesn't. If you are in this category and are bristling at these last words, I suggest getting involved in missions work in the third world (where access to clean safe water and good sanitation is at issue) to recalibrate where you draw the line between desires and needs.

3. **Expectations Evolve:** More recently, psychologists and researchers have looked more deeply into the nature of expectations that progress to the point of being viewed as entitlements - "I deserve this!"

The general consensus is that this is a form of narcissism and is at the root of the frustration and unhappiness among today's younger generation which researchers say is 50% more likely than those over age 60 to feel that they are owed and are special.

What many believe is at the root of this is that the "baby boomers" were raised to believe that hard work would result in a good life. They found that their expectations for life were exceeded and instilled optimism in their offspring. They also fostered a shift from being secure to also being fulfilled at work and an expectation of greater success than their parents or peers. The subsequent generations often feel they are entitled to respect and reward without the hard work that earns them. The result is often short of the expectations and is amplified more recently by the what is referred to as the taunting of "social media image crafting" where others portray themselves as phenomenally successful. As described in the preceding section, the result can go so far as anger at society as a whole for not giving them what they feel they deserve. At this point one begins to feel they are a victim of society and that some part of society is responsible for their victim status as described in the preceding section. They tend not to understand that you become "special" in society through achievement. The Bible in 1 Timothy 5:8 faults those who do not provide for their households as denying their Christian faith. This is at the heart of the work ethic upon which America was founded. Researchers conclude that this is having a negative impact on their relationships with others and ultimately with their own contentment.

Experts tend to view entitlement as the polar opposite of gratefulness, which we have stressed repeatedly in this book is part of the foundation of contentment.

4. **Being Offended:** Again more recently we also see a dramatic increase in discontent triggered by being offended by something. Experts tell us this ties to the preceding discussion on entitlement and feeling special. If you are special and worthy of respect it is difficult to accept that others may hold different opinions. It is difficult to engage in discussions with those who offend you because you want to avoid conflict at any cost as discussed in the opening paragraph of this section. The advice above was to engage, but the usual result is that you demand that authorities shield you from the conflicting views. Refer back to the discussion earlier in this chapter on your reaction to things and how to engage to resolve, rather than avoid conflict. The decision to be offended is just that, a conscious decision. You chose to be offended.

This is not some new development in society; one need only refer to the Bible in John 6:61 where Jesus, feeling the need to speak the unwelcome truth to a crowd says, *"Does what I say offend you?"* The result, the Bible recounts, is that a large number of listeners disengaged and left because they were offended.

5. **Instigators:** You should also realize that there are those in society who benefit from causing conflict. This is not something new and was discussed a quarter century ago (1992) in a book by historian and JFK advisor Arthur M. Schlesinger Jr. - The Dis-Uniting of America. In the book he points out that the antithesis of "e pluribus Unum" (the US Motto, "out of many, one) is the actions of those who seek to divide people by any number of different measures (ethnicity, wealth, religion, etc).

He points out that such actions sow the seeds of conflict where people focus on differences and agitate to be separate rather than being one. He referred to this type of conflict as being against "the original theory of America as one people." He warned that, if allowed to continue, it would tend toward fragmenting society. He pointed out that past presidents such as Woodrow Wilson and FDR made the point that "America does not consist of groups" and that those identifying as a group member have "not yet become an American."

Recognition that there are disruptive people "who are able to make a living," "make themselves prominent before the public" and "do not want the patient to get well" is over a century old. Those three observations (in quotes) were made by Booker T. Washington in 1911. If you encounter people caught up in this sort of "dis-uniting" you will recognize them as major sowers of discontent who often portray groups of people as victims of other groups. Their "modus operandi" is to foment conflict among the groups. If you find yourself drawn to this "conflict between them and us" thinking you will likely never find contentment.

The Bible in Proverbs 6:19 states that on of the six things God truly hates is "a person who stirs up conflict." Enough said!

If you wish to research some history on where a "victim mentality" can lead, look at post-WWI Germany and the importance of Hitler making Germans feel they were victims of an unjust international resolution while also finding a target to foment the "us and them," "it's their fault" attitude.

    6. **Confrontation:** Conflict between individuals often arises when one person says or does something that hurts us, beyond just offending us as discussed earlier. How we handle such situations makes all the difference between normal human interaction and conflict.

There is a tendency to either avoid any form of confrontation and just feel hurt or to launch into an angry confrontation (shouting match). Neither of these is a prescription for contentment. Rather than hold such hurts inside it is better to confront the other person to let them know how you feel.

The risk, of course, is that what you say puts them on the defensive and their response is the start of conflict. The key is in developing the ability to confront someone in a non-accusative manner.

This is actually simpler than it might sound as there is a formula for constructing your response. Start by avoiding an immediate response, giving yourself time to compose your reaction.

The first part is to come up with a non-judgmental description of what they have done; a totally factual and non-emotional set of words. This has to be stated in such a way that there is no way to argue with the validity of what is said.

The second part is to identify the way this hurt made you feel, avoiding the word angry. Yes, you may feel angry, but figure out what triggered the anger and use that feeling instead.

Now insert these two parts into this structure "When you (factual description of action), I feel (the non anger emotion you feel)." For anyone who has parented teenagers here is a situation that has likely led to conflict at some point - your child coming home after the agreed upon time. Try this - "When you come home after the time we agreed upon, I am scared that something might have happened to you." The other person cannot argue with either the fact of lateness or what you say you feel.

Now, and this is critical, prepare for their response and do not allow this exchange to become an argument. Whatever the response is, it is essential that your response demonstrates that you heard and understood what they said without judging or refuting its content.

This technique is called "active listening" and is the first step in responding to whatever they said when confronted. It is particularly important to have your response identify the feeling that the other person is communicating. Ideally your response starts with "You feel that..." and not be just a parroting back (reflective listening) of what was said.
Your response is not necessarily agreeing with what was said, but showing the other person that you heard and understood their response. Done properly this technique significantly reduces arguments and conflict and results in greater contentment in your interpersonal relationships. As Sir Isaac Newton said, "Tact is the art of making a point without making an enemy."

7. **Paralinguistics:** One final thought about conflict concerns how we talk to one another face to face. Communications experts tell us that the message we send to those with whom we converse is sent in three ways: the words we chose to say, the paralinguistics (tone of voice and inflection we use), and our body language (showing anger or impatience for example). Studies in the 1960's tried to assign percentages to each element when there is uncertainty about what is being received. Rather than rely on them as fact suffice it to say that most experts agree that less than 10% of the message is received via the words while over 50% is from the gestures and overall body language. The remaining 40% or so is the tone of voice we use.

Understanding this is key to explaining the potential conflicts that can arise between those who communicate with each other a lot like spouses to each other, parents to children and bosses to employees. The sender has a hard time disguising the real message (which may be tinged with feelings of discontent) and the receiver has an easy time understanding it (and reacts with discontent).

Keep in mind that when communications are non visual (body language not observable) the role of the paralinguistic element becomes even more important in interpreting the spoken words to understanding the real meaning. Experts also point out that when there is incongruence among the three elements, the receiver tends to put more weight on the non-verbal elements, particularly when the non-congruent non-verbal messages are repeated.

This is vitally important because other stressors in your life (other things keeping you from being content) can influence the paralinguistics of everything you say. Your overall discontent can come through and introduce conflict into other interactions. The key, obviously, to prevent triggering discontent in others and the resulting conflict is to work on your own underlying source of discontent such as impatience that influence your non-verbal communications.

## Are You Doing What You Prefer To Do?

We previously mentioned finding ourselves doing things that we look forward to doing. Psychologists (especially of the Jungian school) believe that we are hard-wired with preferences for certain mental processes and that when one has the choice of what to do, these preferences influence our behavior. It is generally felt to be stressful when having to follow paths not in consonance with those preferences.

Experts tell us that we have two fundamental mental processes: collecting information about our environment (called perceiving) and making judgments (drawing conclusions) based on those perceptions. We have two different approaches to perceiving – we can collect bits of information and assemble them into a picture or we can intuitively see a big picture.

One is not better than the other since both are essential parts of figuring out the world; we need to pay attention to details (the bits) in life and also take a step back to look at a big picture. We all do both although most people have a preference for one or the other.

Once we have our perceptions we use them to make decisions about what we are going to do. Again, we have two different methods of drawing conclusions; we can apply logical analysis to what we perceive or we can think about different courses of action and conclude which one feels like the best approach. Again we all do both, but generally exhibit a preference for one or the other.

The key element that, for most people, determines our comfort is how we approach the world. We are either a perceiver (we are continually receptive to new information that could change our path forward) or a judger (we like to make a decision or lay out a plan forward and stick with it). The best way to understand this difference is to think about taking a vacation. Would you rather have only a high-level outline and make your schedule and event decisions as you go along. If this would drive you nuts, you are likely a judger and want things planned and decided. If you think that sounds great, but your traveling companion wants things planned to the nearest 15 minutes, you are a perceiver and will not enjoy things as much if your companion prevails. It's hard to be content when you are approaching things in the non-preferred manner.

Likewise, but to a much lesser degree, if you like the big picture approach to perceiving and are being forced to work in details, it is harder to be content. When you find yourself engaged with someone who is assertive about something (think back to the conflict discussion) and you are most comfortable with logical analysis, it is hard to remain calm and content when the other person keeps saying something that just doesn't feel right.

There is one more difference in people's preferences - how you do your best thinking – when do you gain insights or make the best decisions? If these occur when you are alone and you feel like you give up energy being part of a group, psychologists would categorize you as being more introverted. If, on the other hand you perform best and are energized in a group, your personality is more extroverted. Understanding where you fall is important and does not mean that introverts should avoid group activity while extroverts should assure they are a part of some group. You are more content when in an environment consistent with your preference.

Earlier in the book we talked about choices and making decisions. Think about how you make decisions (what feels right versus logical analysis) and what background you draw upon (experience, past parental guidance, education or religious teachings). Ponder for a moment WHY something "feels right" or where you go for the arguments or data to decide through logical analysis. Likely you use some of each decision process. This type of introspection, bringing these factors into open consciousness and keeping them there is incredibly important in the future decision-making you will undertake.

Rotary has a test (called the 4-Way Test) that members are asked to apply in their decisions of what to say or do: 1. Is it the truth? 2. Is it fair to all concerned? 3. Will it build goodwill and better friendships? 4. Will it be beneficial to all concerned? It is a good test for anyone. Note that attempts to separate people into victims and victimizers is the antithesis of this.

It is important to remaining content that you recognize these inherent differences among the important people in your life and appreciate the difference, rather than fight it. I like to remain open to new information and do my best thinking when alone. I like to start with a big picture for gathering information and then apply rigorous logical analysis. Experts say that only 2% of the population has this combination the way I do, so I must, of necessity, operate in environments beyond my preferences in dealing with family, friends and co-workers. I remain content by realizing that others have a different perspective and approach and that I can benefit from being around them. Fortunately both my late wife and current wife deal with the world as perceivers and were/are more introverted, so it was, and is, easier to be content in those relationships.

## What Motivates You?

There is a school of study that suggests that each of us is motivated to seek self-gratification and that there are a limited number of things that sculpt the nature of our relationships.
This approach teaches that there are only three underlying motivations: the desire to be helpful, the desire to control things and people, and the desire to be analytical and find meaning. Most people would be driven by some strong combination of two and a smaller number by a balance of all three. A very limited number are driven solely by a single motivation.

When you think about what brings you gratification, you begin to see a clearer picture of who you are and what your ideal life could be.

You tend to be more content when the things you do are consistent with your underlying motivations and your desires are gratified. Getting in touch with these motivations helps immensely in doing things that lead to contentment.

I personally am really content when searching out new knowledge (that is the perceiving preference at work) and then analyzing it and fitting it into what I know (that is the analytical motivation at work).

From the discussion on preferences, you have already guessed that I like to do all this while alone. My analytical motivation is coupled with a helping motivation which brings me contentment when I am teaching others or improving the lot of vulnerable children. I do not have a significant desire to control although some could suggest that my love of flying comes from a total desire to control motion in three dimensions – in reality it probably comes from a desire for adventure (which is not addressed in these models of preference or motivation).

The helping motivation is also a driver in wanting to make others happy and deriving gratification from doing so. As a Boy Scout leader for 20+years I always enjoy a quote from the founder of the movement - Robert Baden-Powell:

> *"The most worth-while thing is to try to put happiness into the lives of others."*

# Goals and Striving

You may be thinking "I have goals that I am striving to achieve. Isn't discontent with the status quo the strongest motivation to strive?"

My answer is simply "No, I don't think it is"

Being content with where you are and what you have is not inconsistent with having a plan for the future and desires. We introduced this earlier in the section on conflict. Here is the big question - do you think achieving those goals will make you much happier?

If the answer is yes then I refer you back to chapter one of this book and the quote from Socrates over 2000 years ago:

*"He who is not contented with what he has,*
*would not be contented with what he would like to have."*

The answer is that the goals toward which you are striving may be worthy, but if you don't feel content in the present with efforts toward more education, a nicer lifestyle, or whatever it is you seek, then it is not likely that achieving that goal will bring the happiness you think it will. If your thinking and striving is filled with thoughts of:

## "If only I had....."

then your striving is not toward contentment, but toward an illusory solution to satisfying your desires. You fool yourself into believing that contentment will arrive when you have "the next thing." Think about this:

> If you are striving to get more money, ask why do you want more money. What will happen when you have more money? In all likelihood the answer is I will then be content. So the real goal is finding contentment and you believe that more money is the route to finding it.

I am betting you are still having trouble here - shouldn't I be striving for self-improvement? "If I don't strive, I will become complacent and stop growing." **The answer is clearly yes.**

The right answer here is that they are not contradictory. Take the case of Gandhi who led major cultural change in India. Here are two separate quotes of his:

*"Man's happiness really lies in contentment."*

*"Healthy discontent is the prelude to progress."*

Are they contradictory? Not really. Gandhi felt discontent for the social system in India and strove to change it while being content with himself and his own life. Some would say that his inner contentment gave him the strength to accomplish what he did. If he really was content, then the authorities he faced could not do anything to him that changed that inner strength. Elsewhere in this book I talk about my observations working with those living in the slums of Africa and their attitudes. They confirm this view.

Think about the role that your deepest desires play in how you live your life. There is some philosophy in the Harry Potter stories when he encounters the Mirror of Erised (if you missed it, Erised is Desire spelled backwards like the reflection in a mirror). The mirror shows your life with your heart's greatest desire satisfied. A truly content and satisfied person would see only their own reflection in the mirror.

Harry is warned that there is a danger in prolonged gazing into the mirror in that, while having dreams is good, if one is consumed with what they want they waste their life by forgetting to live and never find happiness.

In a 2018 Rowling inspired movie there is a comment that a character can be trusted to do the right thing because he is not motivated by seeking power or prestige. So sad so many are.

Pretty deep stuff for a children's book, don't you think?

Some may feel that contentment involves being at peace with oneself and the world around us. A major calling in religion is for Peace On Earth. Philosophical discussions of what prevents peace on earth are often not unlike discussions of what prevents inner peace or contentment. The Italian Renaissance scholar Petrarch (1304-1374), by many considered the founder of Humanism, offered a succinct answer in consonance with the thoughts in this chapter. It is interesting that his conclusions did not stray from religious teachings while today's secular humanism posits that religion need not be the foundation of ethics and morality. Think about the motivations of those in history most noted for the disruption of peace among men and nations and how the same attributes keep you from finding inner peace or contentment.

*Five great enemies to peace inhabit within us:*
*Avarice, Ambition, Envy, Anger and Pride.*
*If these enemies were to be banished,*
*We should infallibly enjoy perpetual peace.*

The worst cases of discontent are what experts would call clinical depression that can even lead to suicidal thoughts. Experts suggest that the main causes of suicidal tendencies are: feeling isolated, feeling life is meaningless, feeling like a societal outcast, inability to be oneself around others, adoption insecurity, empty nest syndrome, and a past of familial incest. Clearly combat experiences or PTSD fit in here somewhere.

### In A Word

Through this retrospective, you should understand what truly brings you happiness. You should understand the potholes in the pathway to contentment and have some strategies and tactics for navigating around them. You should better understand your preferences and your motivations.

# Chapter 5:
# Your Life Tomorrow
# You Decide

One of the major elements of the book that Jeri and I wrote about dealing with the loss of one's spouse (<u>Thanks For The Dance - Transforming Grief into Gratitude When Your Spouse Dies</u>) involves rebuilding one's life while dealing with the grief of loss. Much of the material in Chapters 7-9 is applicable here in a non-loss, non-grief environment. The loss of a spouse forces you into a place where you have to think about where you want your life to go and become. Your life was grounded in your relationship with your late spouse; you now have to re-ground your life without that relationship. The only other long term option is to become a hermit and devote the rest of your life to thinking about what you had and what you lost.

The life you plan in the re-building is based on a number of factors and the important point here is that you, right now, are in a position to decide on where you want to go from here. What do you want your re-grounding to look like? Remember the retrospective discussion (Chapter 3) on choices that were later changed to head a different direction. With all the retrospection and introspection this book has suggested in the prior two chapters, you are now poised to build a life of greater contentment and make that the destination of your life's journey without a forcing factor like the loss of a spouse. That was the motivation to write this book - you can chose to change. You truly can create your future.

Do you daydream? About what? Maybe that's your inner self-nudging you to head somewhere else. Your mind wanders to where your heart really is. Listen!

## Where are You Headed?

Unless you are totally content with your life (and that is unlikely given that you have continued to read to this point), you have the opportunity to learn from the retrospection and introspection you've just finished.

First - if you change nothing, where are you headed? Remember the quote from Walden in Chapter Three. The greatest tragedy in life would be *"when I came to die, discover that I had not lived."* The message here is that, if you now truly believe that the journey of life has a destination called contentment, you now have an opportunity to set your GPS to that new destination.

Chapter Two focused on contentment in your relationship with God. It tried to capture thousands of years of wisdom on the life you should live to find that contentment. Hopefully there was something there that made you think about how you can reset your destination.

Chapter Three focused on a retrospective of your life and the degree to which you've been content with the journey you've taken to this place in time. Hopefully you have a new life perspective from thinking about the things about which you are most proud, the regrets for things you did or didn't do, the degree to which you have taken full advantage of the gifts you have been given, and the nature of the choices and decisions you made to get where you are today. All of these are part of the formula for planning where you are headed. You have to learn from the past.

Chapter Four focused on the things that keep you from being totally content with your life today. Hopefully it made you more aware of all the things bringing discontent into your life on a day-to-day basis. Hopefully it gave you some ideas of changes that would keep some of those things out of your life or at least minimize the impact that have on your level of contentment.

This chapter is not going to rehash all of the potential learning from the prior chapter, but to entreat you to look at the notes you jotted down when the text suggested you do so. All of these are part of laying out the pathway for your life tomorrow and beyond. Recall the words of Lao Tzu around 550 BC:

> *"When I let go of what I am,*
> *I become what I might be."*

Ponder for a moment what you are truly seeking in life. If you seek fame or fortune you need to heed the 2500-year-old advice of Psalm49: 17 "They can't take it with them; fame and fortune all get left behind." There must be something more worthwhile to seek. In my youth it seemed that the gurus were saying you needed to find yourself. They should have paid more attention to this (incorrectly attributed to George Bernard Shaw) quote:

> *"Life isn't about finding yourself.*
> *Life is about creating yourself."*

As promised (and hinted at) in the prior chapters, this chapter is going to expand on some other important concepts and tools for planning the pathway forward toward the destination of contentment. It is not too late to create yourself anew and become what you might be. There are six main ideas put forth here:

1. Are you tuned into your passions and are you pursuing them?
2. Are you forming expectations and making them into self-fulfilling?
3. Can you make serendipity happen in your life?
4. Are you truly doing the things that bring everyone happiness and contentment? Has your life truly mattered to others?
5. Are you still carrying things from your past, feelings that eat at you, that cause dis-content?
6. Do you take everything too seriously? Can you laugh in adversity?

## Pursuing Your Passions

Experts contend that most people have never devoted any significant amount of time truly thinking about their passions, no less planning on how to pursue them. A survey of professionals recounted in the 1997 book <u>True Professionalism</u> disclosed that at most 25% truly loved what they do ("This is why I do what I do"). The saddest statistic was that up to 70% responded that they could tolerate what they did ("It's OK, it's what I do for a living"). The remainder, of course, hated what they did. Another survey done by the magazine Fast Company found that only 33% said they were challenged by meaningful work while 55% said they were either "cheerfully engaged" or had "steady un-challenging work." The remainder were either bored or found their work mundane. Think about which category you fall in. If you aren't in the one quarter to one third, then what follows may make a real difference in your life.

In an earlier chapter we mentioned Joseph Campbell and his emphasis on bliss. His exhortation to "follow your bliss" involved finding the things about which you are passionate and putting yourself on a track toward living the life you ought to be living. We emphasize this point in <u>Thanks For The Dance</u> as one of the keys to rebuilding one's life after the loss of a spouse. The model is valuable in any situation where you want to figure out your life's path forward. As part of my consulting and training activities, I developed a model (The Passion Plot™) many years ago and I think it may be of value to you at this point in your life.

The basic concept is to think about things you devote your time and energy to – the things you feel compelled to do because of the pleasure and satisfaction they bring. These are the things where you naturally gravitate when you have the freedom of choice to spend your time, as you want.

We call them passions because of that compulsion to do them.

They are the things that bring us the greatest happiness.

An important element of recognizing them involves the dimension of time – there never seems to be enough time to do them as much as you want and when you are doing them, time seems to fly by. This second tendency can also be explained as becoming lost in doing them – you lose all sense of time. There is a maxim that captures this state of mind

> **"When you find yourself lost in your work,
> you have found your work."**

In other words, you are pursuing a passion if you lose track of time in following it.

This applies to all aspects of your life – work, hobbies, family activities, volunteer work, etc. In Thanks For The Dance we point out that after losing a beloved spouse, you may feel that you will never love life again. We ask if this what your late spouse would have wanted for you? (The answer is "almost certainly not!) It is important that you figure out how to love life.

Confucius was right when he said,

**"Choose a job you love,
and you will never have to work a day in your life."**

People who are bored with life have likely never found their passions – being bored means you have too much time and not enough to fill it. There is perhaps nothing as sad in life as living it without having connected with and pursued one's passions.

For those who have read or seen Tuesdays With Morrie you will likely recall Morrie's philosophy on aging – those who long for their youth are likely leading unfulfilled and unsatisfying lives because they have yet to find the meaning in their life. Embracing your passions is part of finding that meaning. Morrie was right when he said that relationships with family and friends form the foundation of life's meaning.

Those who have connected with their passions find life exciting and moving too quickly with not enough time to do all they want. We hope you can spend the rest of your life in this category. This exercise offers a "trick" that should help you immerse yourself even deeper in your passions.

**"And whatsoever ye do, do it heartily"
Colossians 3:23**

A key element of the model is the underlying assumption (a model foundation) that all of us (we, the authors and you, the readers) have, beyond our relationship with God, an underlying passion for our families. Our greatest happiness comes from involvement with family and there always seem to be demands that keep us from spending more time there. When you think about your passions, your thoughts go first to your family (your spouse, your kids, grandkids, parents, siblings, extended family). This is likely the foundation of your being and life. The Passion Plot™ model has your relationship with God and your passion for your family as its foundation, a circle upon which any other consideration of passions is depicted.

If you think about it, you will hopefully realize the real purpose of life, again beyond our relationship with God, is to make the ones we love happy- hence the importance of family as the foundation of our passions. Author Joe Rigney recounts a major revelation in his young life as a newlywed with a tight budget; he was distressed that his wife was "wasting money on candles" and asked a pastor why candles were so important when money was tight - the response was "because she is!" They brought her happiness- the critical lesson.

What we are looking for are those activities, beyond God and family, where we want to devote our time and attention. This should be differentiated from those activities that call to us and demand our attention and time. The power of coming to understand our passions (and there are a lot of people who have never given this any focused thought at all) is that we can take actions to choose a life where we get to pursue them.

Building the Passion Plot™ is a simple exercise.

Come up with three (non-family related) activities or types of activities that really excite you and call to you.

Think about those times when you have been lost in what you're doing or where you long to spend more time.

Your passion may be a very specific type of activity or a general category of similar activities. The reason for picking non-family related activities is because the overwhelming majority of us would pick that and we are trying to find three unique and self-defining attributes. The role of your passion for family will come back in later.

To guide you along this process, here is the building of my personal Passion Plot™.

The three places where I feel pulled toward spending my time are:

    1. Mentoring – I love to teach and look forward to opportunities to do that. I love to guide others in discovering knowledge, building skills, applying their capabilities to getting things done and solving problems. I have always jumped at opportunities to teach a class, tutor my own kids or others in knowledge and values, or do something to help others develop to their full potential. As a consultant, I love to teach adults how to plan and manage projects. As an adult Boy Scout leader, I have loved guiding youth in building skills and cementing their core values. As a Rotary Club volunteer, I have thoroughly enjoyed and looked forward to helping high school seniors who are unable to pass the Ohio standardized mathematics exam and get a thrill when suddenly a light comes on during the tutoring and several years of math all falls into place for them. As a parent, I think the most fun time is launching your kids into the real world ready to succeed and grow. I look forward to chances to mentor and times flies when I am doing it.

2. Creating – I love to come up with new ideas. Recall from Chapter 3 that what I really wanted to be in life (as a teenager) was a research physicist discovering new knowledge about the universe. I love coming up with a new application of knowledge resulting in something that did not exist before. I have always loved challenges that required a creative response, not just a cookbook answer. I love developing a project to make something happen. In my time in the Air Force, I cherished the opportunity to be involved in weapon system development – helping a team create something new and different. I also jumped at the opportunity to create new management organizations to respond to new challenges – even more so to create new business processes upon which those new organizations would be formed. In my first jobs after the Air Force, I jumped at the chance to figure out how to organize activities to capitalize on emerging technologies and how to take those new technologies and turn them into patentable and producible products. I look for opportunities to bring something new into being and lose track of time when doing that. Authoring books has been that kind of experience.

3. Flying – As I discussed in Chapter 3, in my first year of college I discovered flying. My whole world turned upside down (literally) and I devoted myself and my efforts to becoming a pilot. I got my license while still in college and went off to Air Force pilot training where it did not take long to discover the thrill of flying a "fast mover." Becoming a fighter pilot became my overriding ambition and passion. In all the Air Force assignments where I flew fighters I can remember looking forward to every opportunity to be in the cockpit and lamenting how fast each mission went. I remember thinking on many, many occasions as I flew in formation or flew 500 miles an hour a hundred feet off the ground, "I can't believe they are paying me money to do this."

There has never been anything in my life that has come close to the anticipation and reward of flying. I have owned several airplanes in my life – the high point was buying an antique open cockpit biplane (a British Tiger Moth) and flying it for several years. This was a thrill and clearly fulfillment of a passion. In the words of Jonathan Livingston Seagull - "... the idea of flight for the joy of flying."

If you have come up with your three passions in life (besides your family) then you are ready for the real power of the Passion Plot™. Place the three passions into a triangle naming each of the legs for a passion. You have something like this:

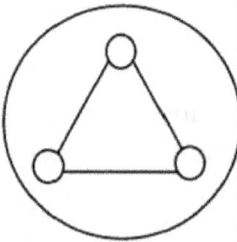

The Passion Plot™
· The circle is the foundation of your family.
· The three sides of the triangle are the passions you identified
· The intersections of the sides are where we focus next

What can we say about the intersections of the passions (the vertices of the triangle)?

Simply that they represent a place where two passions are being satisfied simultaneously.

That sounds like a pretty neat place, doesn't it?

This is where you would like to find yourself as often as possible, doesn't it?

Why not design your path in the direction of some of those passion intersections.

It is a decision you can make.

In addition, think about how you can combine one of the defining passions with the underlying passion for family.

Using my own Passion Plat™ as the example again – this is how I found ways to pursue two passions at once:

Flying and Mentoring: Big surprise – I have held an FAA Flight Instructor License for over 40 years. The biggest thrill in teaching flying is watching the passion erupt in those new to piloting, just as it did for me back in college. My final Air Force flying assignment was as the operations officer of a T-38 Training Squadron. (The T-38 is the "sports car of the Air Force" and the plane that the astronauts use to commute). Getting to teach flying in a plane like this was pure fun for me.

Flying and Creating: How about finding an Air Force job providing a leadership role in creating the F-15E Strike Eagle fighter? How about restoring the Tiger Moth biplane? Pretty obvious direction to go, isn't it?

Mentoring and Creating: You might pause for a moment wondering how to mix these. It is really pretty straightforward – project management is leading teams charged with creating something new. The project manager mentors his team while doing whatever creative stuff the project demands.
I love project management and have made my living as a consultant helping others do it and training them (mentoring/teaching) them how to do it well.

I love to organize and lead projects and I have led several Rotary project to help kids in Africa. The bottom line, whether I am managing an actual project or teaching someone else how to do it, I am in "hog heaven" (whatever that is).

How do these passions relate to my underlying passion for family? I have always loved teaching my kids and grandkids things like reading, math and science. I love helping friends figure out how to be content in their relationship with God (chapter two of this book). I have loved restoring our family home and helping my kids with renovation projects on their homes, creating the perfect place to live. I have loved every opportunity to take family members aloft and let them take the controls of an aircraft. I soloed my late wife in two different airplanes.

As a result of re-evaluating my life and passions following my wife's death I found that a fourth passion (which was always there) was now equal to or greater than flying.

When I was flying combat in VietNam, I was also our squadron's civic action officer responsible for organizing efforts to support a school, orphanage and leper colony. I have looked back on those times as some of the most rewarding things I have done in my life.

I now feel (especially at "my age") that "helping vulnerable children" has surpassed flying in importance since my time flying 500 miles an hour a hundred feet off the ground is a cherished memory and I will likely never own an open cockpit biplane again.

Rebuilding your life by following your passions is an opportunity to do what the Apostle Paul suggests in Romans 12:6-8. We have differing gifts that are likely reflected in our passions and we can use them appropriately. In my case, I can devote my talents (gifts) to helping others.

I have been very blessed to have lived a life of following my passions and routinely and have repeatedly succeeded at satisfying multiple passions simultaneously - I loved the journey as I walked it and am happy now, in retrospect, that I chose that journey to walk.

Being in touch with your passions allows you to have a dream for your life. The song "Happy Talk" in South Pacific sums it up well; "...gotta have a dream. If you don't have a dream, how you gonna have a dream come true?"

I hope that you are able to identify the real passions in your life and lay out a pathway toward contentment as your destination. Remember the foundation for those passions and dreams - your relationship with God and your family.

## Making Expectations Self-Fulfilling

I expect to not be consumed, or even heavily influenced by things that bring discontent. Where I harbor anger or resentment (or worse) I intend to forgive and move on.

What do we really expect out of life?

When you are at a low point (or even a true nadir as discussed earlier) there is no better time to think about our future? Even if things are going well, you have the opportunity to make things even better - to set the expectation that you will achieve contentment as the destination in your life's journey.

Author Lisa Butler wisely observed, "Life is a limited time offer. The best thing is that you get to choose how to use it. It's like a gift certificate that you can spend on anything you want."

As we set our expectations for our future, it is essential to understand that there has been a massive amount of psychological study done on the power of expectations. The bottom line of those studies, supported by a lot of experimental evidence, is that the expectations we set for ourselves and for others tend to become self-fulfilling prophecies. The results of those studies are captured in a body of knowledge called the Pygmalion (or Rosenthal) Effect (much can be found on the internet about this if you are interested.)

The key thing about expectations discussed in the Rosenthal Effect is that when you treat someone as what they could potentially become, we end up facilitating them becoming what they should be. When you hold the same expectations about yourself, the same is true.

Think back to the job satisfaction statistics cited at the start of the passion discussion. What is your expectation from your job? If you set expectations of doing things you love and your work being meaningful and fulfilling, you will subconsciously see opportunities and make choices that take you that direction. Think back to the "potholes" discussion in Chapter 4 where we talked about conflict and the expectation that one's work would be fulfilling. Not loving what you do and the expectation that your work should be fulfilling is automatic dis-content. The earlier discussion pointed out that feeling that one deserves these things (entitled to them) and that one should have them because one is "special" is not the same as setting expectations and doing things that make them "self-fulfilling prophecies."

It is important that you reflect on the discussion in the conflict section of chapter 4 with respect to those places where desires have evolved into expectations where you feel someone else has responsibility to assure they are satisfied. The positive growth expectations where we are talking about in this section are fully your responsibility. Setting expectations is an important first step, but it is not the solution. More on this in the following section on serendipity.

Henry Ford said it well, "Whether you think that you can, or that you can't, you are usually right." If you re-direct your life toward contentment, you will likely succeed in achieving it.

## Making Serendipity Happen

All too often, we do not take time to really think about what has made us the happiest and where our passions really lie. We often do not think in terms of being able to navigate in the direction of greater happiness, bliss and contentment. We are so busy reacting to life and doing the things we have to do that we miss the opportunities to follow a promising path. We may not even recognize that a path presenting itself heads somewhere we really want to go. We think that truly happy people are lucky in that great opportunities have clearly stood in the middle of the road with waving arms to get their attention. We also sometimes think that fortunate, but accidental, discoveries lead others on happier paths.

This is not the reality you may think it is. We need to prepare ourselves to recognize the opportunities. Joseph Campbell, in his famous interviews with Bill Moyers, pointed out that "following your bliss" (pursuing the things about which you are passionate) results in meeting people "in your field of bliss" and the discovery of doors you didn't know were there that will open for you.

As an aside, Joseph Campbell (who studied the myths of many cultures) explained that he came to the embracing of bliss through the ancient Sanskrit word "sat-chit-ananda" defining the jumping off place toward transcendence that comes from your consciousness of being, finding bliss or rapture. He said he wasn't so sure about transcendence, but that following his bliss worked for him.

The key thing you can do, right now, is to stop and think about where you would really like to go – what passions you would love to satisfy. The passion discussion just completed will help a lot in making this a part of your conscious and unconscious thinking.

Think also about the assumptions you hold as sacrosanct truth (these form the basis of your personal paradigms that filter out information that your mind doesn't see as relevant - you never consciously consider it!). One of the keys to experiencing serendipity is a greater openness to information, especially information that you now consider relevant.

You will have prepared yourself to recognize the opportunities when they present themselves. Hinduism's popular god Ganesha, the remover of obstacles, is said to appear out of nowhere to provide just the solution needed. Sounds a lot like what we often think of as serendipity. There is a method here - it is actually a lot easier and reliable than waiting for Ganesha to appear.

It is understanding the role of sagacity in experiencing serendipity.

First, a couple of definitions.

· Sagacity is the ability to observe wisely and to understand and discriminate the relationships inherent in what we observe. The term "Sage" has always referred to someone wise enough to understand what the world around them is saying to them. The sagacious person is able to apply observations and put the parts together usefully.

· Serendipity is the making of unexpected discoveries. The key element is that the discovery was not what was being sought. The word was coined by Horace Walpole in a 1754 letter to Horace Mann based on a fable (The Three Princes of Serendip, 1557) where the characters were able to discover amazing things because their minds were prepared by past experiences to see the connections and the implications.

The essential lesson to be learned here is that we tend to discover things when we have a prepared mind. We are more perceptive of the implications of what we see and what happens around us. We will have developed an internal mental matrix of what is important and are able to see how things around us fit into that matrix in real time. This is the heart of our personal paradigms - if it doesn't fit we tend to subconsciously discard the information as extraneous before becoming overtly aware of it. Broadening one's paradigms makes more information germane to your consciousness.

All too often when disappointed we sit staring at a door that seemingly has seemingly slammed shut in our lives. In so doing we miss the opportunity to see windows or even other doors opening. Without preparation we can fail to see those at all or to comprehend that they have meaning for us. That preparation is the root of sagacity.

Fortunate accidents (serendipitous events) do not just happen to us; we can follow good and wonderful pathways because we now see them and envision where they might lead. The 19th century German philosopher Schopenhauer said: "Talent hits a target no one else can hit; Genius hits a target no one else can see." Anyone can be the genius. Another German, the author Goethe, said that, "The person born with a talent they are meant to use will find their greatest happiness in using it." Artist Paul Cezanne suggested that genius is "the ability to renew one's emotions in daily experience."

The exercises we have outlined in this book such as thinking about the things that have made us proud (Chapter 3) and the Passion Plot™ (this chapter) are part of your sagacity training to help you experience serendipity in life from this point forward. You need to see what was previously unseen.

You may be thinking at this point that this sounds like following your intuition. Albert Einstein, a certified genius who hit targets no one else could see, said, "The intuitive mind is a sacred gift." Experts suggest that intuition is the ability to use patterns that we have already learned. Intuition then is in play whenever we are subconsciously comparing what we are perceiving to what we know.

Experts suggest that our brain function is 20% conscious and 80% non-conscious. The learned patterns are lurking in that 80%. Think back to our discussion on the mental processes of perceiving and making judgments and recall that all of us use both big picture and detailed data as methods of perceiving and use both logical analysis and gut feel as methods of making decisions. Where did the patterns come from? Sometimes it is as simple as some sense of moral right versus wrong instilled in us years before. Sometimes it is a past experience we've since "forgotten" or something we read or saw and stored away "for future reference."

Plato, 2400 years ago, suggested intuition was the ability to comprehend the true nature of reality and is based on all of us having pre-existing knowledge of certain things (some would call this instinct, Plato called it anamnesis). Jung, a hundred years ago, suggested that intuition was perception via the unconscious (so that the patterns form without our conscious action). All of this notwithstanding, there are actually two ways intuition can happen.

1. Think about times when you felt, in your gut, something "just wasn't right" and hesitated a moment to focus on it. What was likely happening was that what you perceived did not fit immediately into the pattern. When you find yourself in situation that has potential danger you feel yourself tingling with warning. Sometimes when you meet someone new, you feel a sense of unease about them. You didn't need to analyze to have a hunch. The other explanation is that that there is some external consciousness (call it your "guardian angel") sending you the "nudge" we talked about earlier in this book. That is how most people explain that gut feeling to delay when the light turns green and, sure enough, someone runs their red light and would have hit you had you moved.

2. Think about times you felt a compulsion to do something and it turned out to be a very fortuitous decision. The potential action fit well into your stored pattern without you having to analyze it. The action may have been to study, explore or find out more and it may have been to do something decisive. A primary role of intuition can be triggering us to search for more information - to add to the existing pattern.

I discussed earlier a couple of my personal nudges or compulsions (joining the grief support group and finding the spot where I now live). I stated that I believe God guided me. Others would suggest that something fit a stored pattern and pushed me to act as I did. I have gobs of cases where I do think the later is the case, just not the ones cited earlier.

3. Think about the times you have read something that gave you a new insight (routine Bible study often does this) and in the next 24 hours encountered something that reinforced it - "whoa, I just read about that."

Being in touch with your sources of passion, pride and happiness is like a new window or door being opened for you. The key is for us to avoid staring so much at closed doors that we miss the new opportunities. These things create the internal pattern against which we subconsciously compare all we encounter. The more mature those patterns are and the more we have thought about them, the more likely it is that opportunities will be seen as fitting nicely. That fits well with the central idea of serendipity - the prepared mind.

## Doing Things That Bring Everyone Happiness

Researchers on the subject of happiness, bliss, joy and contentment tend to agree that there are certain things that produce these feelings. Generosity is key among them.

Psychologist Sonja Lyubromirsky concluded that these are key factors:
· The ability to reframe our current situation positively
· The ability the experience gratitude
· The choice to be kind and generous.

Neuroscientist Richard Davidson contends that there are four main brain circuits that we can activate that result in contentment.

1) The ability to maintain positive states
2) The ability to recover from negative states
3) The ability to maintain focus (avoiding mind wandering)
4) The ability to be generous (feeling good when helping others)

Albert Schweitzer devoted his life to helping others and summarized thusly: "The purpose of human life is to serve, and to show compassion and the will to help others."

The Dali Lama and Desmond Tutu, in The Book of Joy, conclude that there are eight pillars that lead to joy (or in our focus, contentment). At the end of the book they offer practices focused on finding joy or contentment. There are four pillars that focus on the mind and four that focus on the heart. In summary, we should

· Train our minds to place things into perspective (reframe situations to see the positive and the opportunities while understanding that we do not control all aspects of any situation) - The Christian knows Who does and the power of prayer.

· Embrace humility (recognizing that our gifts come from God and celebrating other's gifts),

· Embrace humor (able to laugh at our vulnerabilities and manage anxiety of the unknown), and

· Accept the reality of life (not being anxious about how life should be, not being so reactive - The believer can pause in prayer for guidance and wisdom).

· Focus our heart on forgiveness (not being controlled by the past), the Bible stresses this universal truth repeatedly.

· Focus our heart on gratitude (count your blessings and not your burdens, the Bible tells us to be grateful in all circumstances. Few things are more important to finding contentment than being satisfied with and grateful for all your blessings),

· Focus our heart on compassion (being motivated to help relieve the suffering of others, not just be empathic toward it) and

· Focus our heart on generosity (giving not just money but also your time and talent to help others be happier).

That same book also warns that we cannot pursue joy as an end in itself and offers a great little analogy - if we pursue joy we will miss the bus since it is bringing joy to others that gets us on the bus. The authors kid around saying that money can buy happiness ... if we spend it on others. They expand that explaining that giving is not just money, but also our time. They point out that we are also giving when we help free someone from fear, offer wisdom and moral teachings, and help make others more self-sufficient. They explain a key difference between empathy and compassion - empathy is concern for the plights of others while compassion is the drive to do something about it.

As suggested earlier in this chapter, ask yourself "Has my life really mattered to others?" If the answer is not a resounding yes, then think about how you can make it matter. Think about all those who made a difference in your life, those who helped give your life meaning and purpose. Ask yourself how you can now be the person that you needed in your life years ago. I have found that through my civic action work in VietNam, tutoring high school seniors unable to pass the required proficiency test in math, and work in Africa, and now Ecuador, through Rotary, I feel a deep happiness in having tried to make others' lives better and happier.

An unknown author captured the role of parent and mentor well when he said:

> *"Don't educate your children to be rich.*
> *Educate them to be Happy.*
> *So when they grow up they will know*
> *the value of things not the price."*

Albert Einstein had it figured out:

> *"How strange is the lot of us mortals!*
> *Each of us is here for a brief sojourn;*
> *for what purpose we know not, though sometimes sense it.*
> *But we know from daily life that we exist for other people*
> *first of all for whose smiles and well-being*
> *our own happiness depends."*

So where are you trying to go with your life? What is the plan for the years you have left? I can only return again to the thoughts in Chapter Three and playing around with the words life and living. Is our life measured in the years we live? Is the major activity of life making a living? A pastor named Bob Morehead wrote an essay in 1995 called "The Paradox of Our Age" that you have probably seen quoted. This is my favorite part of his essay:

> *"We've learned how to make a living, but not a life;*
> *we've added years to life, not life to years."*

When we talk about life it is common to refer to the physiological elements that technically define being alive - breathing and your heart beating. So to differentiate between being alive and living I paraphrase poet Phillip Bailey (1853) - We should count time, not by heartbeats, but by heartthrobs.

You've almost certainly heard the 1989 quotation from Vicki Corona (and likely attributed to a host of other people more famous):

*"Remember that life is not measured*
*by the number of breaths we take,*
*but by the moments that take our breath away!"*

So, where are you headed? Do you want to give your journey of life a destination called contentment? Hopefully this chapter has given you pause to reflect and reset your navigation.

## Forgiving

Perhaps you are getting tired of this subject since we have mentioned it throughout the book. If you are truly going to make contentment the destination of your life, then this is one of the keys to making that happen. Remember that forgiveness is both of you and others.

In The Book of Forgiving Desmond Tutu offers what I think is a neat little exercise to focus on the impact on your life of holding on to things that bring you discontent. He suggests finding a palm-sized stone and carrying it around for a full day in your non-dominant hand. At the end of the day reflect on what carrying the stone added to your life and all of the limitations carrying the stone imposed on you. Carrying feelings that prevent contentment (like bitterness, guilt, anger and so forth) that can be eliminated through forgiveness is just like carrying that stone.

I loved the exercise because it points of the futility of dwelling on things in the past that can't be changed and letting them impact your daily life today.

Ask yourself, after you have carried the stone and reflected on the benefits and impacts of carrying it, what do you do with it now. You can keep it as a reminder or you can get rid of it forever - either is a valid action, Tutu suggests.

There will be people in your life that hurt you. Continuing to hold those hurts inside prevents being content. You need to make a conscious decision to rid yourself of those things that are eating at you.

There are perhaps people in your life that you hurt. If you have been carrying guilt, or even shame, with you over those actions, then you need to ask forgiveness. If it is too late (for example, the person has died) then you still need to take some action (such as writing them a letter you never mail) that addresses that regret. The key is seeking forgiveness, even if the person you hurt doesn't offer it. There is also a big opportunity to reflect on whether you are carrying guilt or shame. Guilt is when you realize you have done something wrong or hurt someone while being ashamed is feeling there is something wrong with whom you are. In either case you need to forgive yourself for what you did - I was wrong to do what I did and this is not who I really am.

Experts in holistic healing suggest that internalizing and carrying any form of hurt has negative impacts on our overall health. Holistic alternatives such as Emotional Polarity Technique (EPT™) and Emotional Freedom Technique (EFT™) focus on finding those internalized hurts and eliminating them primarily though forgiveness.

Contentment isn't always easy to come by. Many of us have traumas and negative emotions stemming from these traumas, and we can't find the key to letting go of them and the dis-ease, the pain and discontent they cause us. Contentment and joy are your birthright as a human being.

Learning how to let go and be free to create a new life story is the ultimate goal. Sometimes you need help in releasing those traumas and emotions that no longer serve you or are keeping you stuck, preventing you from living the life you were meant to live. Forgiveness is key and emotional therapies like EPT™ and EFT™, as well as many other holistic therapies can help you release these negative emotions and false beliefs about yourself, someone else, certain situations, or life in general. Learning to love and accept yourself *just as you are* is an important first step to contentment.

In a healthy body, energy flows freely. Emotional and physical traumas can cause blockages which, if unresolved, may lead to dis-ease and negative emotional and behavioral patterns that prevent you from living well and creating what you really want in life. EPT™ and EFT™ teach that the REAL healing comes through forgiving not only those who caused you pain or trauma, but also in forgiving yourself for any false beliefs you have adopted that caused you to hold on to the pain or trauma in the first place. Once you forgive it is much easier to feel gratitude for all that life has taught you. After all . . . Life is the school and LOVE is the lesson! Never stop learning!

EPT™ and EFT™ contend that the people/pets and situations that are placed in our paths are to teach us and provide the exact experiences we need to grow our soul. Be grateful for them and the sometimes difficult lessons they teach us. Healing and learning from these experiences is a part of the lesson. Learning forgiveness, gratitude and above all else, love, is the lesson! And it all starts with learning to love yourself. See yourself as God sees you . . . as perfectly YOU! Once you see yourself through this truth, you can more easily see others in the same light; the light of unconditional love.

If you need help finding healing, holistic emotional therapies are an amazing, effective, gentle and drug free way to get there faster. Holistic therapies go to the root of the issue and heal it directly at the source. The holistic health community is quickly growing as western medicine is failing more an more people with chronic illnesses by pushing addictive, toxic drugs and other "band aids" to cover up the real issues, instead of going to the root of the problem and fixing them at the source.

If you would like more information, some helpful books on the topics are, *The Forgiveness Doctor* by Dr. Annette Cargioli, *The Tapping Solution* by Nick Ortner, and *You Can Heal Your Life* by Louise Hay. These are all a good place to start on your healing journey and understanding how emotions such as anger, fear, and guilt play a huge part in your physical, mental, and spiritual health!

Tutu, in his book, shares his own experience of having had a very abusive father who one day said he needed to talk about something important with him. Tutu reflects on telling his dad he was too tired then and suggested having the conversation in the morning. It eats at him to this day because he thinks his dad wanted to ask forgiveness and his dad died that night. He never had the chance to forgive his dad face to face.

### Ensure Humor Has a Place in Your Life

Do you like to laugh? Do you feel better when laughing? Most would say yes. Comedian/Actor Charlie Chaplain observed that: **"A day without laughter is a day wasted."**

What makes you laugh? Those who analyze things like this suggest it is often that the "punch line" breaks our expectation of where the story or joke is headed.

How do you handle things where your expectation of where life and its events are headed? How about when events flag our own frailties or vulnerabilities?

Humor can be a great vehicle for dealing with anxiety and stress. Medicine tells us that laughter causes the release of endorphins into our system. You may have heard the term "gallows humor." This is witticism in response to a hopeless situation; it treats serious matters lightly or satirically. Experts suggest that it often has a morale boosting effect on those in the bad situation and point out that there is a long history of it in literature. It is an effective method of dealing with adversity. When Sir Walter Raleigh was executed by being beheaded by axe in 1618 among his final words were "This is a sharp medicine." More recently, when Ronald Reagan was shot in 1981 and in the emergency room he said to the ER doctors "I hope you're all Republicans." Gallows humor is common in the military where danger abounds as a mechanism for dealing with seeing death - most combat veterans continue to use dark humor to cope.

Most people don't face the stress in life of someone in combat, but we do face bad times. The ability to joke about it is a real plus. A joke told by Steve Martin illustrates this: "After the tests the doctor said there was good and bad news. The good news is that there will be a disease named after you."

The willingness to make ourselves the "butt of the joke" is a great stress reliever - technically this is called "self-deprecation" and is lot better than aiming humor at others. All of us do silly or embarrassing things from time to time and often would prefer to keep them to ourselves - the ability to laugh about them with others is a great tonic. Laughter shared with others is even better since it is self-reinforcing or infectious.

The Dali Lama (in <u>The Book of Joy</u>) suggests that there are many people who feel they need to be somber to project a sense of "gravitas" or seriousness, thinking that will result in them being more respected. He suggests that the real result is that you are viewed as pompous and suggests that the ability to laugh at yourself is the best antidote for that. Tutu in that same exchange says, "Come stand next to me and let's laugh at me together."

So, find reasons to laugh and get others to laugh with you. Find cartoons that tickle you. Post them where you will see them often. My personal favorites are in "The Far Side" series. As comedian Milton Berle once said:

*"Laughter is an instant vacation"*

It's hard to be discontent when laughing.

### In A Word

As a result of this chapter you should appreciate that your life forward is more of a blank slate than you may have realized. Hopefully you now understand your passions and have a better idea about how to pursue them. You should better understand the power of expectations and how to experience serendipity. You should better appreciate the importance of helping others, forgiving, and having humor in your life.

# Chapter 6

## Your Life in the Moment

I can, at any point in time that I wish, put myself in a position and state of mind where a feeling of contentment flows over me and I want for nothing other than the pleasure (hedonic, eudemonic, and relaxation) of the moment.

Right now I can sit on my porch hugging my wife and petting my rescue dog, while gazing into the woods that surround my house and listening to the sound of the creek below me and the birds around me, while reflecting on how blessed my life has been. Sometimes there are shafts of light in the woods as the sunlight filters through the tree tops. I marvel at the incredible wonder and beauty of God's creation (some refer to this as a "tiny theophany" - seeing God with our senses). The feeling is amazing. All the problems of the day and demands of tomorrow evaporate. Back in Chapter Two I talked about the nudges that led us to find what we still think is one of the most serene places we've ever been. We bought the vacant lot of weeds and built a house on the edge of the drop off to the creek. We are surrounded by woods out every window and the predominant sounds we hear are the creek and birds singing. From the back of the house we can't see any signs of civilization. From the gazebo by the pond we dug, we can look out across the ripples in the water and sound of the fountain causing them. We can watch the sun set over the barn. We were nudged to find a place where we can turn off whatever stresses or demands we feel and just sink into a state of contentment. We are very blessed to call this home and talk of our gratitude daily. We pray that you too will be nudged in the direction of finding that special place to find contentment in the moment.

So....this chapter is about finding contentment in the moment.

Earlier we mentioned the expression "Let Go. Let God." For those who embrace and accept God's sovereignty, these words tell us to let go of our tension and concern over the situations of the moment. My approach in times of stress is to place myself in one of my calm and serene places and to pray for the guidance and wisdom to deal with whatever is troubling me. I open myself to the nudges that aim me on that right path. I am letting go of my angst and letting God guide me.

I promised early in the book that I would explain the cover. It has very great significance for me. It is an antique oil painting I own (one of several I have with a very similar theme - sheep filling the road ahead). When my late wife and I were stationed in England, on more than one occasion we would be driving a narrow country road and come upon a shepherd and his flock going the same direction we were and completely filling the road. These events changed my overall thinking about impatience and dis-content. I could be angry and frustrated about being delayed and moving at the sheep's pace OR I could be peaceful in the moment with a situation I could not change. I chose to be content in the circumstance (remember where that phrase comes from?). The decision to be content in the moment changed my life and I have told the story of sheep in the road for decades since. The first time I took my new wife Jeri to England I reflected on the experience of many years before and thankfully we found ourselves following a flock of sheep and the experience became real for her as well.

You may well have experienced a similar situation and this is a good time to think about how you reacted. Have you ever been on the Interstate when you come to a complete stop and that stop continues for an hour or more. There is likely a serious accident ahead and all lanes have been closed. The longest I have waited in this situation is two and a half hours.

What have you observed and how have you felt. The most recent experience of mine saw cars driving down the right shoulder to get ahead of the two mile backup. After they came to a halt, more cars came by to the right of them on the grass next to the shoulder and they too came to a halt. After a while they forced their way across the three lanes of stopped traffic and drove down the left shoulder against traffic looking for a way to cross the median. While I sat and listened to pleasing music and surfed the web on my phone I felt sorry for those impatient folks. I thought to myself "how sad it would be to be them." No anger, just contentment in the moment.

I cannot stress enough here that the ability to become content in the moment is absolutely essential to finding contentment in life. There is another saying I have heard that may apply to those who will never find themselves behind a flock of sheep on a narrow English road - "Enjoy The Detour." How do you react when finding a road closed and being forced to take an alternate route?

Do you feel frustration and a need to get back on the intended route as soon as possible? You can change your life by changing your reaction or response to finding yourself on an alternate route - not just in driving, but anytime life takes you a direction not in accordance with your plans. Sometimes the detour is short and other times you never return to the pathway you were following (like when your spouse of many years dies and you need to rebuild your life). When the detour is short, force yourself to gain an appreciation of the way you are now going and find enjoyment in that part of the trip.

Longfellow had some really sage advice worth considering

*"The best thing one can do when it's raining is to let it rain."*

I personally agree even more with Vivian Greene, whose observation was fully applicable to our earlier book <u>Thanks For The Dance</u>.

> *"Life's not about waiting for the storms to pass*
> *It's about learning to dance in the rain"*

That thought is the foundation of the Serenity Prayer with which everyone is likely familiar. ("God grant me the **serenity** to accept the things I cannot change; **courage** to change the things I can; and wisdom to know the difference.")

There is another key fact about finding contentment in the moment - when you are under stress, when you are impatient, when you are angry, you tend to make decisions or take actions that are not well thought out. Being dis-content leads to sub-optimal (if not totally bad) decisions. This was reinforced to me in USAF pilot training; when facing an emergency situation (airplanes do break while airborne) the first step is ALWAYS to calmly analyze the situation BEFORE taking action. This is a place where a bad decision can kill you.

One of my life's heroes, nicknamed "Pop," was a combat medic in World War II and made six Pacific Theatre beach landings in the first or second wave. He was tending wounded on the beach at Iwo Jima when the flag went up. He had a gratitude-based response whenever things were stressful - "Well, at least they aren't shooting at us!" I have added that to my list of pithy responses.

So, here is what you need to do

1. Have a place you can go where you can disconnect yourself from whatever is bringing you any form of discontent. Spend time there appreciating where you are and not focused on anything but being content.

2. Develop the ability to clear your mind of any stressors that lead to discontent. There are two dimensions to this ability.

> The first is to focus on everything for which you are grateful -this is the most effective way to disconnect from discontent. Offering prayers of gratefulness or thanksgiving for the entire blessing you have brings great calming.

> The second is to practice forgiveness. If your discontent comes from reaction to what others have done, forgiving them takes a load off your mind. If your discontent comes from regrets you harbor, forgive yourself for that action or inaction, and move on. It is very hard to move forward when you are looking rearwards at the things you regret.

And, here are two things that I think are not at all effective, but still popular. Work on the two responses above and avoid these.

- Find something to do that takes your mind off the situation causing discontent. In our book <u>Thanks For The Dance</u> we point out the futility of engaging in frenetic activity to mask or hide from your grief at your loss. Such activity may temporarily divert you from the situation but it will not lead you where you need to go - contentment.

-Drugs that offer an escape from stress. This is a one-way street going in the wrong direction. This is not the route to contentment on your journey.

In my younger days I remember all the admonitions to find peace and joy through meditation. The practice of Transcendental Meditation, Zen, and even the Beatles finding their guru who would bring them inner peace seemed at the hippy edge of things.

In reality, the ability to meditate, to calm your bodily reactions to stress, and to escape make more sense to me today than way back then. I think that the avenue to contentment is much simpler than what was embraced back then. Thank God for all the blessings you have and marvel at His creation.

I need to repeat here what was said in an earlier chapter because this is where they all come together. Contentment in the moment comes from listening to the music and the sounds of nature that you love, being grateful that you are living a life filled with purpose and meaning and filled with loving others and making the ones you love happy, understanding how best to make full use of your God-given talents in "following your bliss," and being able to relax physically and mentally in the midst of stress and turmoil.

---

Japanese culture has a word for this - IYASHI

癒

Where one finds warm solace, peace, harmony and balance

---

I find Iyashi offering my daily prayers of gratitude, seeing a beautiful sunrise through the woods with shafts of light through the mist among the trees, while hearing the sounds of singing birds, feeling my rescue dog snuggled against me and smelling and tasting a freshly brewed espresso. That pretty well covers all the senses. True contentment results from marveling in, and being grateful for the wonder of God's creation and thanking Him for all the blessing I have received.

As an aside and not surprisingly, the Japanese have a word for the shafts of light (in English they are referred to in cold scientific terms as crepuscular rays) - in Japanese they are:

## KOMOREBI (木漏れ日)

Author C.S. Lewis provided an interesting discussion on these rays of light in a 1945 essay. He points out that normally we do not see light - we see the things that light illuminates. He was taken by a sunbeam shining into a dark toolshed and the fact that the focus of his attention was the light (and the reflection off the dust particles in the air). He went on to philosophize about the difference between looking at and looking along (into) the light - he saw no toolshed or beam of light. If light is the metaphor for God, there is a difference in our lives from seeing evidence of the light and looking along the light toward its source (knowing God personally).

Hopefully now you will stop, marvel, and redirect your thoughts into a state of Iyashi the next time you encounter Komorebi. Maybe take the time to read Psalm 104. Contemplate what C.S. Lewis said about the deeper meaning.

Later C.S. Lewis explained in his 1960 book "The Four Loves," that we can both seek pleasure or unexpectedly encounter something that brings us pleasure. In the first case we desire something pleasurable, we seek it and find it, and, satisfied, move on. (Think being thirsty and getting a drink of water) In the later case the unexpected encounter brings both pleasure and appreciation (a form of love), we tend to praise it and be grateful (rejoice) that it exists. We may also feel the desire to preserve it for others to enjoy as well. Lewis also suggests that beyond the gratitude for the beauty of God's creation and our enjoyment of it, one should also feel a sense of adoration for the creator. Contentment from looking both "at" and "along."

To this point, Albert Einstein once remarked: "Joy in looking and comprehending is nature's most beautiful gift."

Experts suggest that our greatest contact with our intuition occurs while in this state. Remember in our earlier discussion that intuition is felt to be a conscious reflection of what we perceive against the 80% of our mental function where learned patterns reside. Without a flurry of conscious activity about what going on in the world and all of our reasons to be discontent (the noise of daily living), we can hear what the inner voice is saying.

It is a good time to experience both of the dimensions of intuition - the "something's not right here" and the "now I see how that fits in."

The practices and exercises in the final chapter of The Book of Joy are all directed toward placing yourself in a contented state "in the moment." All of these begin with finding a place where you can get comfortable, focusing on and controlling your breathing (each breath in brings calming and each breath out exhales stress), and becoming contemplative. One of the techniques recommended is to keep a journal where every day you note three things for which you are grateful.

Once calm and contemplative I find the greatest contentment comes from rejoicing in the day and all the blessings that came with it. There is a simple guide to doing this put together by St Ignatius of Loyola (1491-1556, the founder of the Jesuit order) called the Daily Examen. He suggests reflecting on your day with particular attention to the emotions you are feeling, then accepting the experience of the day and expressing gratitude for it. This puts you in the place to rejoice in today and to look forward to tomorrow.

May you find that right place and may you figure out how to re-orient your thoughts to find contentment in the moment as you work on setting contentment as your destination. The Bible (Ecclesiastes 4:6) reminds us that is better to have one handful of something with tranquility or quietness than to have two handfuls with toil, travail, and vexation of spirit. Being content in the moment, and recognizing the importance of that contentment over having more, is essential.

The Apostle Paul in the Bible used this word many (29) times;

## φρονέω

It is Greek and pronounced phroneo and is generally translated into English as "set your mind upon." The stronger meaning is giving one's ultimate attention and affection to something, it becomes a value upon which your thoughts and deeds are based. Paul's many exhortations include: humility, meekness, patience, forgiveness, thankfulness, being honorable and being truthful.

### In A Word

You should realize the importance of being able to find contentment in the moment and have some ideas about how to do this in our own life.

# Chapter 7

## *Final Thoughts*

The preceding six chapters were my best effort to convince you that the destination of a life's journey should be contentment and then to define the nature of contentment. I have tried to differentiate among feelings such as joy, happiness and contentment and elements of living such as needs, wants, and desires, and to explain the power of expectations and of being prepared to better see the paths toward contentment. Before providing a list of "one-liners" from the book let me say a few final words about needs, wants, and desires and their role in setting one's expectations. Understanding the difference between needs and wants was found in the quote from Epictetus (circa 100AD) that:

## *"Wealth comes from having few wants"*

And the admonition from Socrates five hundred years earlier that:

## *"He who is not contented with what he has, would not be contented with what he would like to have."*

So, I have found in my life that I am content if:

1. My needs are met.
>    My needs are:
>>    A.  God's Pleasure at:
>>>    What is in my heart

How well I have loved others
How well I have used the talents given
me
    B.  Life sustaining air, water, food, shelter

2. My wants and desires are satisfied.
    My most important wants and desires are:
        A.  Contentment in my relationship with God.
            That I will feel God's presence in guiding
            my life
        B.  Contentment in the life I have lived and am
living.
            That I will be constantly grateful for all
            my blessings
            That I have brought and bring happiness
            to those I love.
            That I have been the friend that others
            needed
        C.  Having the ability to be content in the
            moment
        D.  That I have helped others find the
            contentment I have

3. This earthly/mortal life I am living brings me pleasure

    My sources of this pleasure and my relationships are:

        A. My Spouse: I am so grateful to God that she
            exists, that God guided me to meet her,
            and that we found each other.

B. My 4 kids and 8 grandkids: I am so grateful to God to have them (including the seeming miracles surrounding the two adoptions and the pregnancies that occurred coincident with the adoptions). I thank God for the opportunities I have had to influence their beliefs and values and to "train them up in the way they should go" to the best of my ability (with God's help)

C. My Friends: I am so grateful to God to have discovered people who share the same truths with me and that we want to support and nurture each others' walks in this life.

D. Nature: I am so grateful to God for the complexity, delicacy, interplay, and beauty of His creation. I stand in awe of nature and the creator

E. Art: (also known as earthly stuff - the paintings, needlework, well crafted furniture, sculpture, architecture, poetry, music, etc): I am so grateful to God for the talent given to the artists who made these earthly things and for my place in time owning (their temporary custodian), seeing, hearing these things for my brief instant in eternity.

4. My expectations are met.
   My expectations are:
   A. I will be able to continue to grow and mature in my relationship with God.

B. God will continue to bless my life and those I love

C. I will be able to continue to follow my passions

D. I will remain satisfied and grateful for my remaining days

E. I will be able to avoid those things that bring dis-content

F. I will be able to find contentment even when things are challenging

G. I will cling to true friends and nurture true friendship.

## LOVE

The word love is used over a hundred times in this book. The ancient Greeks had six different words. Love deserves a short section here. The best essay on the subject has been mentioned earlier ("The Four Loves" by C. S. Lewis in 1960 near the end of his life). Lewis initially thought the subject would be straight-forward; the Bible tells us that "God is Love" and all other discussions would flow from this. He sees that God gifts love to us in many ways and then realizes that this doesn't explain our need for love. He agrees with St. Augustine that to love makes us vulnerable; especially loving something you might lose.

The section in Chapter 4 on loneliness (one of the potholes preventing contentment) explains that it results from our need for others throughout our lives. Lewis points out that we come to God in prayer when we need something or help. He summarizes this "need-love" as needing someone "to tie up what is dangling and to untie what has become tangled or knotted."

The prior discussion of the Lewis book in Chapter 6 explains the difference between finding pleasure in having a need met and the pleasure in encountering (unsolicited) something that we appreciate (resulting in Appreciative Love). The values discussion in Chapter 3 on our love of our country is a form of appreciative love- because "our country" is ours.

There are numerous places where we discuss wanting to make others happy - this is affection, what Lewis called the "humblest love." Appreciative love is usually a basic element of affection - we appreciate those toward whom we feel affection. Importantly we both want to gift affection toward others and crave (need) their affection. We need to be needed (if only by our pet animal). Lewis suggests that affection is responsible for 90% of what makes us happy. Realizing that one is un-needed or un-appreciated is one of the greatest sources of unhappiness and a discontented life.

Lewis offers an amazing discussion on friendship (philia) much in keeping with the Francis Bacon quote in Chapter 4. He points out that in ancient society, friendship was considered "the happiest and most human of all loves" and that friendship arises from two (or more) people having the epiphany "What! -You Too?" discovering that they share a belief in the same truths or are both "on the same secret road." Lewis posits that true friends help each other in rough times and that gratitude, mentioned so often in this book, is not a major factor ("Don't mention it" the common exchange).

Lewis then explores the inevitable "Eros" where he differentiates between sensual pleasure (sexual desire) and someone else being "beloved." The first is about your own needed and sought pleasure and the other is about giving.

The final love that Lewis explores is Charity (Agape)- a form of "Divine Gift Love" - firstly, to love what is naturally unlovable (no appreciate, affection, or friendship). It is also love of God to whom you can give nothing that is not already His. The love we receive from God is this first type of charitable love. Lewis suggests that anytime we find ourselves saying "If only..." we have an opportunity to practice charity.

One final thought on love - this one from Jonathan Livingston Seagull, a book about the love of flying (that I obviously relate to). Jonathan reflects how he has sought the nature of love and concluded that the true nature of love is wanting to forgive others (the flock of gulls who had banished him) and be kind. He also felt that the best way to demonstrate love is to give something of the truth he has seen to others.

**So, here are my one-liners for:**

## Putting Your Life On The Journey Toward Contentment

- Work on the relationship with God - make that the core of your being. As C.S. Lewis said - this is the first thing.

- Believe that your life is being guided. Hope that μετάνοια (metanoia) happens to you and that you come to γινώσκω (ginosko) this - not just believe it. Remember what Einstein said about coincidence.

- Be alert for the nudges to take a specific path or do a certain thing.

- Don't ask for God's intervention to make things turn out the way you want.

- Do ask for God to provide you with strength, courage and wisdom.

- Do offer prayers of thanksgiving constantly for all the blessings you receive.

- Marvel daily in the wonder and beauty of God's creation - enjoy them, recognizing their source.

- Learn to appreciate and give thanks for all the good moments.

- Savor all of the positive experiences of your life.

- Look for the growth or beneficial outcome resulting from life's low spots. Know that God meant them for good. Figure out how.

- Get in touch with your passions.

- Figure out how to live your life pursuing your passions.

- Don't ever let "more money" be the deciding factor in your life decisions.

- Don't make material wealth a significant goal in your life.
- Believe that doing what you love results in all the worldly success you will ever want

- As you acquire material things, appreciate them for what they are and NOT for what they are worth. Don't focus on getting a lot of material possessions, but try to surround yourself with material things that mean a lot to you.

- Minimize "If only...." thinking. It traps you in a past that can't be changed. Recognize "if only..." as an opportunity for "agape love."

- Recognize that regrets only diminish your contentment - let go of them.

- Forgive yourself for regrets over things you've done or didn't do.

- Forgive others for things that impacted you - release the power they have over you.

- Set your expectations and make them self-fulfilling.

- Prepare yourself so you recognize opportunities that take you where you want to go.

- Laugh more and share laughter with others.

- Come up with some short statement that captures your core goal in life and say it often to those important to you. (Mine is "Make the ones you love happy.")

Take time every day to sit quietly and reflect on your gratefulness. Search for surroundings and companionship that makes the feeling of gratefulness grow even stronger. Find a place where this reflection can be the most intense and most long lasting. Marvel at the wonder of God's creation. Let that result in becoming more in awe of God.

If you have reached this point annoyed (or at least incredulous) at the idea of being grateful in all circumstances, allow me to add the thoughts of a military leader - Admiral Nimitz on Christmas Day 1941 taking over the Pacific Command after Pearl Harbor. He was grateful the attack happened on a Sunday since tens of thousands of men were ashore and not on the ships sunk, that the attack did not damage the dry docks hence allowing ship repairs to be done in Hawaii, and that the attack did not take out the entire Pacific fuel supply in the open just 5 miles from Pearl Harbor.

I hope this book has given you pause to think and the tools to figure out how to set contentment as your destination.

Keep in mind the quote from Marcus Aurelius (circa 180 AD):

### *"Very little is needed to make a happy life; it is all within yourself, in your way of thinking."*

And....remember what Lao Tzu said 2500 years ago:

### *"Contentment is The Greatest Treasure."*

I will leave you with the Dali Lama's response to what surprises him most. It is that:

*"Man sacrifices his health in order to make money. Then he sacrifices money to recuperate his health. And then he is so anxious about the future that he does not enjoy the present; the result being that he does not live in the present or the future; he lives as if he is never going to die, and then dies having never really lived."*

I wish you:

1. A life of loving what you do,
2. A life of being grateful for life's blessings
3. A life of heartthrobs, not just heartbeats
4. A life that is breathtaking
5. A life of contentment

So I will end with Jonathan Swift's blessing quoted earlier:

*"May you live all the days of your life."*

www.ingramcontent.com/pod-product-compliance
Lightning Source LLC
Chambersburg PA
CBHW072010040426
42447CB00009B/1564